PRENTICE HALL

Realidades Ⓐ

Guided Practice
Activities

D1535632

PEARSON

Prentice
Hall

Needham, Massachusetts
Upper Saddle River, New Jersey

3 4 5 6 7 8 9 10   08 07 06 05

ISBN 0-13-116472-4

Table of Contents

Para empezar

Tema 1: Mis amigos y yo

Tema 2: La escuela

Tema 3: La comida

Tema 4: Los pasatiempos

Dear Parents and Guardians:

Learning a second language can be both exciting and fun. As your child studies Spanish, he or she will not only learn to communicate with Spanish speakers, but will also learn about their cultures and daily lives. Language learning is a building process that requires considerable time and practice, but it is one of the most rewarding things your child can learn in school.

Language learning calls on all of the senses and on many skills that are not necessarily used in other kinds of learning. Students will find their Spanish class different from other classes in a variety of ways. For instance, lectures generally play only a small role in the language classroom. Because the goal is to learn to communicate, students interact with each other and with their teacher as they learn to express themselves about things they like to do (and things they don't), their personalities, the world around them, foods, celebrations, pastimes, technology, and much more. Rather than primarily listening to the teacher, reading the text, and memorizing information as they might in a social studies class, language learners will share ideas; discuss similarities and differences between cultures; ask and answer questions; and work with others to practice new words, sounds, and sentence structures. Your child will be given a variety of tasks to do in preparation for such an interactive class. He or she will complete written activities, perform listening tasks, watch and listen to videos, and go on the Internet. In addition, to help solidify command of words and structures, time will need to be spent on learning vocabulary and practicing the language until it starts to become second nature. Many students will find that using flash cards and doing written practice will help them become confident using the building blocks of language.

To help you help your child in this endeavor, we offer the following insights into the textbook your child will be using, along with suggestions for ways that you can help build your child's motivation and confidence—and as a result, their success with learning Spanish.

Textbook Organization

Your child will be learning Spanish using *REALIDADES*, which means "realities." The emphasis throughout the text is on learning to use the language in authentic, real ways. Chapters are organized by themes such as school life, food and health, family and celebrations, etc. Each chapter begins with a section called **A primera vista** (*At First Glance*), which gives an initial presentation of new grammar and vocabulary in the form of pictures, short dialogues, audio recordings, and video. Once students have been exposed to the new language, the **Manos a la obra** (*Let's Get to Work*) section offers lots of practice with the language as well as explanations of how the language works. The third section, **¡Adelante!** (*Moving Ahead!*), provides activities for your child to use the language by understanding readings, giving oral or written presentations, and learning more about the cultural perspectives of Spanish speakers. Finally, all chapters conclude with an at-a-glance review of the chapter material called **Repaso del capítulo** (*Chapter Review*), with summary lists and charts, and practice activities like those on the chapter test. If students have trouble with a given task, the **Repaso del capítulo** tells them where in the chapter they can go to review.

Here are some suggestions that will help your child become a successful language learner.

Routine:
Provide a special, quiet place for study, equipped with a Spanish-English dictionary, pens or pencils, paper, computer, and any other items your child's teacher suggests.

- Encourage your child to study Spanish at a regular time every day. A study routine will greatly facilitate the learning process.

Strategy:

- Remind your child that class participation and memorization are very important in a foreign language course.
- Tell your child that in reading or listening activities, as well as in the classroom, it is not necessary to understand every word. Suggest that they listen or look for key words to get the gist of what's being communicated.
- Encourage your child to ask questions in class if he or she is confused. Remind the child that other students may have the same question. This will minimize frustration and help your child succeed.

Real-life connection:

- Outside of the regular study time, encourage your child to review new words in their proper context as they relate to the chapter themes. For example, when studying the vocabulary for the household chapter, Level B, Capítulo 6B, have your child help with household chores and ask him or her to name the tasks in Spanish. You could also have your child label household objects with adhesive notes containing the Spanish words. Similarly, while studying Level A, Capítulo 4A vocabulary, have your child bring flash cards for place names on a trip into town and review words for the buildings you pass along the way. If your child can include multiple senses while studying (see the school and say *escuela*, or taste ice cream and say *helado*), it will help reinforce study and will aid in vocabulary retention.
- Motivate your child with praise for small jobs well done, not just for big exams and final grades. A memorized vocabulary list is something to be proud of!

Review:

- Encourage your child to review previously learned material frequently, and not just before a test. Remember, learning a language is a building process, and it is important to keep using what you've already learned.
- To aid vocabulary memorization, suggest that your child try several different methods, such as saying words aloud while looking at a picture of the items, writing the words, acting them out while saying them, and so on.
- Suggest that your child organize new material using charts, graphs, pictures with labels, or other visuals that can be posted in the study area. A daily review of those visuals will help keep the material fresh.
- Help your child drill new vocabulary and grammar by using the charts and lists in the **Manos a la obra** and **Repaso del capítulo** sections.

Resources:

- Offer to help frequently! Your child may have great ideas for how you can facilitate his or her learning experience.
- Ask your child's teacher, or encourage your child to ask, about how to best prepare for and what to expect on tests and quizzes.
- Ask your child's teacher about the availability of audio recordings and videos that support the text. The more your child sees and hears the language, the greater the retention. There are also on-line and CD-ROM based versions of the textbook that may be useful for your child.
- Visit www.PHSchool.com with your child for more helpful tips and practice opportunities, including downloadable audio files that your child can play at home to practice Spanish. Enter the appropriate Web Code from the list on the next page for

the section of the chapter that the class is working on and you will see a menu that lists the available audio files. They can be listened to on a computer or on a personal audio player.

Capítulo	A primera vista	Manos a la obra	Repaso
Level A			
Para empezar			jcd-0099
Capítulo 1A	jcd-0187	jcd-0188	jcd-0189
Capítulo 1B	jcd-0197	jcd-0198	jcd-0199
Capítulo 2A	jcd-0287	jcd-0299	jcd-0289
Capítulo 2B	jcd-0297	jcd-0298	jcd-0299
Capítulo 3A	jcd-0387	jcd-0388	jcd-0389
Capítulo 3B	jcd-0397	jcd-0398	jcd-0399
Capítulo 4A	jcd-0487	jcd-0488	jcd-0489
Capítulo 4B	jcd-0497	jcd-0498	jcd-0499
Level B			
Capítulo 5A	jcd-0587	jcd-0588	jcd-0589
Capítulo 5B	jcd-0597	jcd-0598	jcd-0599
Capítulo 6A	jcd-0687	jcd-0688	jcd-0689
Capítulo 6B	jcd-0697	jcd-0698	jcd-0699
Capítulo 7A	jcd-0787	jcd-0788	jcd-0789
Capítulo 7B	jcd-0797	jcd-0798	jcd-0799
Capítulo 8A	jcd-0887	jcd-0888	jcd-0889
Capítulo 8B	jcd-0897	jcd-0898	jcd-0899
Capítulo 9A	jcd-0987	jcd-0988	jcd-0989
Capítulo 9B	jcd-0997	jcd-0998	jcd-0999

Above all, help your child understand that a language is not acquired overnight. Just as for a first language, there is a gradual process for learning a second one. It takes time and patience, and it is important to know that mistakes are a completely natural part of the process. Remind your child that it took years to become proficient in his or her first language, and that the second one will also take time. Praise your child for even small progress in the ability to communicate in Spanish, and provide opportunities for your child to hear and use the language.

Don't hesitate to ask your child's teacher for ideas. You will find the teacher eager to help you. You may also be able to help the teacher understand special needs that your child may have, and work together with him or her to find the best techniques for helping your child learn.

Learning to speak another language is one of the most gratifying experiences a person can have. We know that your child will benefit from the effort, and will acquire a skill that will serve to enrich his or her life.

Notes

Write the Spanish vocabulary word below each picture. If there is a word or phrase, copy it in the space provided. Be sure to include the article for each noun.

Buenos días.	**Buenas noches.**	**Buenas tardes.**
_____ _____	_____ _____	_____ _____
¡Hola!	**¿Cómo te llamas?**	**Me llamo...**
_____	_____ _____	_____ _____
Encantado, Encantada.	**Igualmente.**	**Mucho gusto.**
_____, _____	_____	_____

Realidades Ⓐ

Para empezar

Nombre _____

Hora _____

Fecha _____

Vocabulary Flash Cards, Sheet 2

¿Cómo está Ud.?	¿Cómo estás?	¿Qué pasa?
¿Cómo _está_ _Ud.?_	_¿Cómo_ _estás?_	_¿Qué_ _pasa?_
¿Qué tal?	¿Y tú?	¿Y usted (Ud.)?
¿Qué _tal?_	_¿Y_ _tú?_	_¿Y_ _usted (Ud.)?_
(muy) bien	regular	gracias
(muy) _bien_	_regular_	_gracias_

Realidades (A)

Para empezar

Nombre _____

Hora _____

Fecha _____

Vocabulary Flash Cards, Sheet 3

nada	señor, Sr.	señora, Sra.
_____	_____,	_____,
señorita, Srta.	**¡Adiós!**	**Hasta luego.**
_____, _____	_____	_____
Hasta mañana.	**¡Nos vemos!**	**uno**
_____ _____	_____ _____	_____ _____

dos _____	**tres** _____	**cuatro** _____
cinco _____	**seis** _____	**siete** _____
ocho _____	**nueve** _____	**diez** _____

Realidades **A**

Para empezar

Nombre _____

Hora _____

Fecha _____

Vocabulary Flash Cards, Sheet 5

¿Qué hora es?

___ ¿Qué ___

___ hora ___

___ es? ___

[1:00]

Es ___ la ___

___ una ___ .

[2:00]

Son ___ las ___

___ dos ___ .

[3:05]

Son ___ las ___

___ tres ___ y ___

___ cinco ___ .

[4:10]

Son ___ las ___

___ cuatro ___ y ___

___ diez ___ .

[5:15]

Son ___ las ___

___ cinco ___ y ___

___ cuarto ___ .

[6:30]

Son ___ las ___

___ seis ___ y ___

___ media ___ .

[8:52]

Son ___ las ___

___ ocho ___ y ___

___ cincuenta ___

___ y ___ dos ___ .

[6:40]

Son ___ las ___

___ seis ___

___ menos ___

___ veinte ___ .

Realidades **A**

Para empezar

Nombre _____

Hora _____

Fecha _____

Vocabulary Flash Cards, Sheet 6

_____

_____

_____

_____

_____

_____

_____

_____

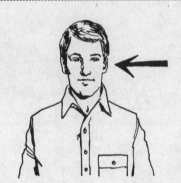

_____

_____

_____

_____

_____

_____

_____

_____

_____

_____

Tear out this page. Write the English words on the lines. Fold the paper along the dotted line to see the correct answers so you can check your work.

En la escuela

Buenos días.   _____

Buenas noches.   _____

Buenas tardes.   _____

¡Hola!   _____

¿Cómo te llamas?   _____

Me llamo...   _____

Encantado,
Encantada.   _____

Igualmente.   _____

Mucho gusto.   _____

señor, Sr.   _____

señora, Sra.   _____

señorita, Srta.   _____

¡Adiós!   _____

Hasta luego.   _____

Hasta mañana.   _____

¡Nos vemos!   _____

Fold In →

Tear out this page. Write the Spanish words on the lines. Fold the paper along the dotted line to see the correct answers so you can check your work.

Good morning. _____

Good evening. _____

Good afternoon. _____

Hello! _____

What is your name? _____

My name is . . . _____

Delighted. _____

_____

Likewise. _____

Pleased to meet you. _____

sir, Mr. _____

madam, Mrs. _____

miss, Miss _____

Good-bye! _____

See you later. _____

See you tomorrow. _____

See you! _____

Fold In →

Vowel sounds

• Like English, Spanish has five basic vowels, **a, e, i, o**, and **u**. But unlike English, each Spanish vowel sounds nearly the same in every word, which will help you figure out how to pronounce any Spanish word you see.

A. The letter **a** is pronounced "ah," as in the English word "father." Write three Spanish words related to *body parts* (**el cuerpo**) that contain the letter **a**. Say each word as you write it, paying special attention to the **a**.

_____   _____   _____

B. The letter **e** is pronounced "ay," as in the English word "pay." Write three Spanish *numbers under ten* that contain the letter **e**. Say each word as you write it, paying special attention to the **e**.

_____   _____   _____

C. The letter **i** is pronounced "ee," as in the English word "see." Write two Spanish words used in *greetings* that contain the letter **i**. Say each word as you write it, paying special attention to the **i**.

_____   _____   _____

D. The letter **o** is pronounced "oh," as in the English word "go." Write three Spanish *numbers over ten* that contain the letter **o**. Say each word as you write it, paying special attention to the **o**.

_____   _____   _____

E. The letter **u** is pronounced "oo," as in the English word "zoo." Write three Spanish words that you've learned so far that contain the letter **u**. Say each word as you write it, paying special attention to the **u**.

_____   _____   _____

Realidades Ⓐ

Para empezar

Nombre _____

Hora _____

Fecha _____

Guided Practice Activities P-2

The letter c

- The letter **c** has two different sounds in Spanish. When it is followed by **a**, **o**, **u**, or any consonant other than **h**, it is a "hard **c**" and is pronounced like the **c** in "cat." Say these words with a hard **c**:

    <u>c</u>ómo   prá<u>c</u>tica   en<u>c</u>antado

- When the letter **c** is followed by **e** or **i**, it is a "soft **c**" and is pronounced like the **s** in "Sally." Say these words with a soft **c**:

    do<u>c</u>e   gra<u>c</u>ias   silen<u>c</u>io

A. Write out the numbers below (which all contain at least one letter **c**) in Spanish on the blanks provided.

1. 4   _____

2. 0   _____

3. 13   _____

4. 100   _____

5. 11   _____

6. 5   _____

7. 16   _____

8. 14   _____

9. 55   _____

10. 48   _____

B. Now, say aloud each of the words you wrote, paying special attention to the letter **c**. Go back to the answers you gave in **part A** and underline each hard **c** (as in **c**at). Circle each soft **c** (as in **S**ally). **Ojo:** Some words contain more than one **c**.

Realidades Ⓐ

Para empezar

Nombre _____

Hora _____

Fecha _____

Vocabulary Flash Cards, Sheet 1

Write the Spanish vocabulary word below each picture. If there is a word or phrase, copy it in the space provided. Be sure to include the article for each noun.

el *bolígrafo*	la *carpeta*	el *cuaderno*
el *estudiante*	la *estudiante*	la hoja de *papel*
el *lápiz*	el *libro*	el *pupitre*

Realidades **A**

Para empezar

Nombre _____

Hora _____

Fecha _____

Vocabulary Flash Cards, Sheet 2

la sala
de clases

el
año

el
día

el
mes

la
semana

¿Qué día
es hoy?

¿Cuál es
la fecha?

Realidades

Para empezar

Nombre _____

Hora _____

Fecha _____

Vocabulary Flash Cards, Sheet 3

Es el primero de enero. _____ _____ _____ _____	**Es el tres de marzo.** _____ _____ _____ _____	**Es el cinco de mayo.** _____ _____ _____ _____
Es el catorce de febrero. _____ _____ _____ _____	**Es el once de septiembre.** _____ _____ _____ _____	**Es el veinticinco de diciembre.** _____ _____ _____ _____
mañana _____	**hoy** _____	**en** _____

¿Cuántos?, ¿Cuántas? _____ ,	**hay** _____	**por favor** _____
¿Cómo se dice...? _____ _____	**Se dice...** _____ _____	**¿Cómo se escribe...?** _____ _____
Se escribe... _____ _____	**¿Qué quiere decir...?** _____ _____ _____	**Quiere decir...** _____ _____

Tear out this page. Write the English words on the lines. Fold the paper along the dotted line to see the correct answers so you can check your work.

En la clase

el bolígrafo _____

la carpeta _____

el cuaderno _____

el estudiante, _____
la estudiante

la hoja de papel _____

el lápiz _____

el libro _____

el profesor, _____
la profesora

el pupitre _____

la sala de clases _____

el año _____

el día _____

el mes _____

la semana _____

hoy _____

mañana _____

Fold In

Realidades Ⓐ

Para empezar

Nombre _____

Fecha _____

Hora _____

Vocabulary Check, Sheet 2

Tear out this page. Write the Spanish words on the lines. Fold the paper along the dotted line to see the correct answers so you can check your work.

pen _____

folder _____

notebook _____

student _____

_____

sheet of paper _____

pencil _____

book _____

teacher _____

_____

(student) desk _____

classroom _____

year _____

day _____

month _____

week _____

today _____

tomorrow _____

Fold In →

More c sounds

- In **Activity P-2** you learned that the letter **c** has two different sounds in Spanish: "hard **c**" and "soft **c**." The "hard **c**" sound is also created by the letter groups **que** and **qui**. **Que** is always pronounced like the English "kay" and **qui** is always pronounced like the English word "key." Say these words:

  quince   que   quiere

A. Remember that the hard **c** is sometimes spelled with a **c** and sometimes with a **q**. Underline the words in each group below with a hard **c** ("cat") sound. Say each word aloud as you read it.

1. clase / García / doce

2. trece / cien / carpeta

3. equis / cierren / dieciséis

4. gracias / saquen / Cecilia

5. cero / silencio / catorce

6. once / cuaderno / diciembre

B. Circle the words in each group with a soft **c** ("Sally") sound. Say each word aloud as you read it.

1. Ricardo / cuarto / atención

2. diciembre / cómo / octubre

3. carpeta / cuaderno / Alicia

4. qué / quiere / decir

5. cien / Cristina / cuántos

6. saquen / cierren / capítulo

Realidades (A)

Para empezar

Nombre _____

Fecha _____

Hora _____

Guided Practice Activities P-4

The *h* sound

- In Spanish, some letters have different pronunciations than they do in English. For example, the letter **j** is pronounced like the letter *h* in the English word "**hat**," but even more strongly and in the back of the throat. The letter **g**, when followed by **e** or **i**, also has the same "h" sound. However, the Spanish letter **h** is always silent! Say these words aloud:

  Jorge   **jueves**   **hay**   **hasta**   **hoja**

A. Circle all of the words below with a *pronounced* "h" sound. Don't be fooled by the silent letter **h**! Say each word aloud as you read it.

julio	hoy	hasta
~~h~~oja	Jorge	Juan
junio	Guillermo	hora
José	página	hay
juego	¡Hola!	Eugenia

B. Now, go back to the words in **part A** and draw a diagonal line through every silent **h**. The first one has been done for you. Did you notice that **hoja** has both a silent **h** and a **j** that has a *pronounced* "h" sound?

Realidades

Para empezar

Nombre _____

Hora _____

Fecha _____

Vocabulary Flash Cards, Sheet 1

_____

_____

_____

_____

_____

_____

_____

_____

_____

_____

_____

_____

_____

_____

_____

_____

_____

_____

Realidades Ⓐ

Para empezar

Nombre _____

Hora _____

Fecha _____

Vocabulary Flash Cards, Sheet 2

_____ _____	**la estación** _____ _____	**¿Qué tiempo hace?** _____ _____ _____
_____ _____	_____ _____	_____ _____
_____ _____	_____ _____	_____ _____

Realidades (A)

Para empezar

Nombre _____

Hora _____

Fecha _____

Vocabulary Check, Sheet 1

Tear out this page. Write the English words on the lines. Fold the paper along the dotted line to see the correct answers so you can check your work.

El tiempo

Hace calor.   _____

Hace frío.   _____

Hace sol.   _____

Hace viento.   _____

Llueve.   _____

Nieva.   _____

la estación   _____

el invierno   _____

el otoño   _____

la primavera   _____

el verano   _____

Fold In →

Realidades Ⓐ

Para empezar

Nombre _____

Hora _____

Fecha _____

Vocabulary Check, Sheet 2

Tear out this page. Write the Spanish words on the lines. Fold the paper along the dotted line to see the correct answers so you can check your work.

It's hot.   _____

It's cold.   _____

It's sunny.   _____

It's windy.   _____

It's raining.   _____

It's snowing.   _____

season   _____

winter   _____

fall, autumn   _____

spring   _____

summer   _____

Fold In

To hear a complete list of the vocabulary for this chapter, go to Disc 1, Track 1 on the Guided Practice Audio CD, or go to www.phschool.com and type in the Web Code jcd-0099. Then click on **Repaso del capítulo.**

Realidades Ⓐ

Para empezar

Nombre _____

Hora _____

Fecha _____

Guided Practice Activities P-5

Special letters

- When studying the alphabet, you will notice a few letters that you may not have seen before. In addition to the letters we have in English, Spanish also has **ll**, **ñ**, and **rr**.

  a) **ll** is pronounced like a "y" in English, as in the word "**y**ellow."

  b) **ñ** is pronounced like the combination "ny," as in the English word "ca**ny**on."

  c) **rr** is a "rolled" sound in Spanish. It is made by letting your tongue vibrate against the roof of your mouth, and sounds a bit like a cat purring or a child imitating the sound of a helicopter.

Look at the pictures below and fill in the blanks in the words or phrases with either the letter **ll**, **ñ**, or **rr**. Be sure to say each word aloud as you write it, practicing the sounds of the new letters.

1. Es la se_____ora Guité_____ez.

4. _____ueve en la primavera.

2. Me _____amo Gui_____ermo.

5. Hace viento en el oto_____o.

3. Es el libro de espa_____ol.

The letters *b* and *v*

- In Spanish, the letters **b** and **v** are both pronounced with a "b" sound, like in the English word "**boy**." This makes pronunciation simple, but can make spelling more challenging! Say the following words:

  Buenos días.   **¡Nos vemos!**   **brazo**   **veinte**   **bolígrafo**   **verano**

The phrases below all contain either **b** or **v**. Pronounce both with a "b" sound, and write the correct letter in the blanks in each conversation.

1. —Hola, profesor.

   —_____uenos días, estudiantes.

2. —¿Qué tiempo hace en el otoño?

   —Hace _____iento.

3. En fe_____rero hace mucho frío.

   —Sí, hace frío en el in_____ierno.

4. —¿Qué tiempo hace en la prima_____era?

   —Llue_____e pero hace calor.

5. —¿Qué día es hoy?

   —Hoy es el _____einte de no_____iembre.

6. —Le_____ántense, por fa_____or.

   —Sí, profesora.

7. —¿Cómo estás?

   —_____ien, pero me duele el _____razo.

Write the Spanish vocabulary word below each picture. If there is a word or phrase, copy it in the space provided. Be sure to include the article for each noun.

Realidades Ⓐ

Capítulo 1A

Nombre _____

Hora _____

Fecha _____

Vocabulary Flash Cards, Sheet 3

sí

_____

_____ _____ _____

_____ también y

_____ _____ _____

pues... ni... ni o

_____ _____ _____

Realidades Ⓐ

Capítulo 1A

Nombre _____

Fecha _____

Hora _____

Vocabulary Flash Cards, Sheet 4

Realidades (A)

Capítulo 1A

Nombre _____

Hora _____

Fecha _____

Vocabulary Check, Sheet 1

Tear out this page. Write the English words on the lines. Fold the paper along the dotted line to see the correct answers so you can check your work.

bailar _____

cantar _____

correr _____

dibujar _____

escribir cuentos _____

escuchar música _____

esquiar _____

hablar por
teléfono _____
_____

ir a la escuela _____

jugar
videojuegos _____
_____

leer revistas _____

montar en
bicicleta _____
_____

montar en
monopatín _____

Fold In

Nombre _____ Hora _____

Fecha _____ **Vocabulary Check, Sheet 2**

Tear out this page. Write the Spanish words on the lines. Fold the paper along the dotted line to see the correct answers so you can check your work.

to dance _____

to sing _____

to run _____

to draw _____

to write stories _____

to listen to music _____

to ski _____

to talk on
the phone _____
_____

to go to school _____

to play
video games _____
_____

to read magazines _____

to ride a
bicycle _____
_____

to skateboard _____
_____

Fold In

Tear out this page. Write the English words on the lines. Fold the paper along the dotted line to see the correct answers so you can check your work.

nadar   _____

pasar tiempo   _____
con amigos
                                _____

patinar   _____

practicar deportes   _____

tocar la guitarra   _____

trabajar   _____

usar la   _____
computadora
                                _____

ver la tele   _____

                                _____

Fold In

Realidades Ⓐ

Capítulo 1A

Nombre _____

Hora _____

Fecha _____

Vocabulary Check, Sheet 4

Tear out this page. Write the Spanish words on the lines. Fold the paper along the dotted line to see the correct answers so you can check your work.

to swim _____

to spend time
with friends _____

_____

to skate _____

to play sports _____

_____

to play the guitar _____

to work _____

to use the
computer _____

_____

to watch
television _____

Fold In

To hear a complete list of the vocabulary for this chapter,
go to Disc 1, Track 2 on the Guided Practice Audio CD, or
go to www.phschool.com and type in the Web Code jcd-0189.
Then click on **Repaso del capítulo.**

Infinitives (p. 36)

- The most basic form of a verb is an *infinitive*.
- In English, infinitives have the word "to" in front of them such as *to walk* or *to swim*.
- In Spanish, infinitives end in **-ar** (nadar), **-er** (leer), or **-ir** (escribir).

A. Look at each infinitive below and underline its ending. Follow the model.

| Modelo | patin<u>ar</u> |

1. escrib<u>ir</u>	4. esqui<u>ar</u>	7. le<u>er</u>
2. nad<u>ar</u>	5. us<u>ar</u>	8. jug<u>ar</u>
3. corr<u>er</u>	6. dibuj<u>ar</u>	9. v<u>er</u>

B. Now, write the infinitive in the correct column of the chart. Is it an **-ar** verb, **-er** verb, or **-ir** verb? The first one has been done for you.

-ar verbs	*-er* verbs	*-ir* verbs
patinar		

C. Complete the sentences with infinitives from **part A** to express what you like and don't like to do.

1. Me gusta _____ y _____ .

2. No me gusta _____ .

3. Me gusta mucho _____ .

Negatives (p. 42)

- To make an English sentence negative, you usually use the word "not": *I do **not** like to sing.*
- To make a Spanish sentence negative, you usually put **no** in front of the verb or expression: *No me gusta cantar.*
- To answer a Spanish question negatively, you often use **no** twice: **¿Te gusta bailar?** *No, no me gusta.*
- To say that you do not like something at all, you add the word **nada**: **No, no me gusta** *nada.*
- To say you don't like either of two choices, use **ni... ni**: **No me gusta** *ni* **correr** *ni* **practicar deportes.**

A. Look at the sentences and circle only the *negative* words you see. Some sentences do not have negative words. Follow the model. (*Hint:* There should be eight words circled.)

Modelo ⓃⓄ me gusta cantar.

1. ¿Te gusta bailar?

2. No, no me gusta bailar.

3. ¿Te gusta patinar?

4. No, no me gusta nada.

5. No me gusta ni bailar ni patinar.

B. You circled three different negative words in **part A** above. What are they? Write them on the lines.

_____ _____ _____

C. Use the negative words **no, ni,** and **nada** to complete the following conversation.

ELENA: Enrique, ¿te gusta escuchar música?

ENRIQUE: No, _____ me gusta.

ELENA: ¿Te gusta bailar?

ENRIQUE: _____, no me gusta bailar.

ELENA: No te gusta _____ escuchar música _____ bailar. ¿Qué te gusta hacer?

ENRIQUE: ¡Me gusta ver la tele!

ELENA: ¡Uy, no me gusta _____!

Go Online WEB CODE jcd-0104
PHSchool.com

Realidades Ⓐ

Capítulo 1A

Nombre _____

Hora _____

Fecha _____

Guided Practice Activities 1A-3

Negatives (continued)

D. Complete the sentences with activities you don't like. You can use the drawings for ideas of activities.

1. No me gusta _____.

2. No me gusta _____.

3. No me gusta ni _____ ni _____.

E. Now answer the questions negatively. Follow the models.

Modelos ¿Te gusta esquiar?
No, no me gusta esquiar.

¿Te gusta correr y nadar?
No, no me gusta ni correr ni nadar.

1. ¿Te gusta dibujar?

_____

2. ¿Te gusta cantar?

_____

3. ¿Te gusta escribir cuentos?

_____

4. ¿Te gusta esquiar y nadar?

_____

5. ¿Te gusta patinar y correr?

_____

Expressing agreement or disagreement (p. 44)

- To agree with what another person <u>likes</u>, use **a mí también**:
  —Me gusta patinar.
  —**A mí también.**
- To agree with what another person <u>dislikes</u>, use **a mí tampoco**:
  —No me gusta cantar.
  —**A mí tampoco.**

A. The word web shows positive (agreement) words and negative (disagreement) words that you have learned. Look at the sample conversation, paying attention to the words **también** and **tampoco**. One of these two words is positive and one is negative. Write each word in the correct circle of the word web.

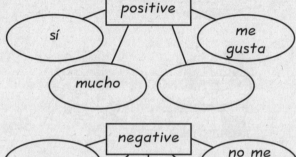

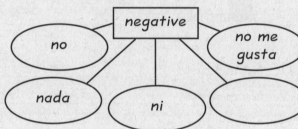

JUAN: A mí me gusta correr.
ANA: A mí **también**.
JUAN: No me gusta cantar.
ANA: A mí **tampoco**.

B. Now, complete the following exchanges with either **también** or **tampoco**.

1. JORGE: A mí me gusta mucho dibujar.
   SUSANA: A mí _____.

2. LUIS: No me gusta nada hablar por teléfono.
   MARCOS: A mí _____.

3. OLIVIA: A mí no me gusta ni bailar ni correr.
   ALBERTO: A mí _____.

4. NATALIA: Me gusta esquiar. ¿Y a ti?
   JAVIER: A mí _____.

5. SARA: A mí no me gusta trabajar.
   PABLO: A mí _____.

6. LORENA: Me gusta mucho montar en bicicleta. ¿Y a ti?
   MARTA: A mí _____.

C. Look back at the exchanges in **part B** above. Put a plus (+) next to the exchange if it is positive. Put a minus (–) next to it if it is negative.

Go Online WEB CODE jcd-0105
PHSchool.com

Lectura: ¿Qué te gusta hacer? (pp. 46–47)

A. The reading in your textbook contains four self-descriptions by students from various parts of the Spanish-speaking world. Read the following selection about Marisol. Then answer the questions that follow.

|| *"¿Te gusta practicar deportes y escuchar música? ¡A mí me gusta mucho! También me gusta jugar al básquetbol. ¡Hasta luego!"* ||

1. Go back to the reading above and circle the sentence where Marisol is asking you a question.

2. Underline the words that tell you that Marisol is talking about things that she likes.

3. Now list the activities that Marisol likes to do in the spaces below:

_____   _____   _____

B. Read the following selection written by Pablo and answer the questions that follow.

|| *"Me gusta mucho jugar al vóleibol y al tenis. Me gusta escribir cuentos y también me gusta organizar fiestas con amigos. No me gusta ni jugar videojuegos ni ver la tele. ¡Hasta pronto!"* ||

1. Underline the words that tell you that Pablo is talking about things that he likes.

2. Circle the things Pablo does not like.

3. Pablo is from «Guinea Ecuatorial». How would you write that in English?

_____

C. Some quotes from the reading are listed below. Identify the speaker of each by writing in their name and country of origin. Follow the model.

Modelo   "Me gusta jugar al básquetbol." __*Marisol*__ __*Puerto Rico*__

1. "Me gusta mucho ver la tele." _____ _____

2. "Me gusta escribir cuentos." _____ _____

3. "Me gusta hablar por teléfono con amigos." _____ _____

4. "Me gusta organizar fiestas con amigos." _____ _____

5. "Me gusta tocar el piano." _____ _____

Realidades A

Capítulo 1A

Nombre _____

Hora _____

Fecha _____

Guided Practice Activities 1A-6

Presentación oral (p. 49)

Task: Pretend that you are a new student at school. You have been asked to tell the class a little bit about your likes and dislikes.

A. Fill in each empty space in the diagram with at least two activities that represent you.

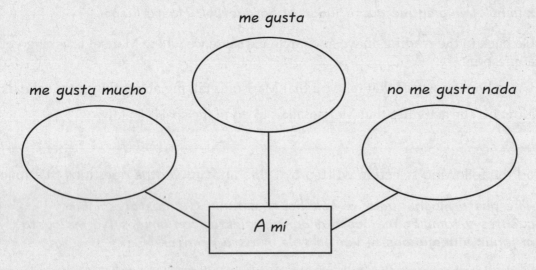

me gusta

me gusta mucho

no me gusta nada

A mí

B. As part of your presentation, you will need to introduce yourself to everyone before you begin talking about your likes and dislikes. Think about how you would introduce yourself in Spanish to someone you don't know. Write one possibility below.

_____

C. Now, add to your greeting by talking about what you like and dislike. Using your information from the diagram in **part A**, write three sentences describing what you like, what you like a lot, and what you do not like.

1. Me gusta _____.

2. Me gusta mucho _____.

3. No me gusta _____.

D. Your teacher will always evaluate your presentations using a rubric, which is like a checklist of elements needed to perform your task. The fewer items completed, the lower the score. Some of the items for this presentation include:

- how much information you communicate
- how easy it is to understand you
- how clearly and neatly your visuals match what you are saying

Realidades Ⓐ

Capítulo 1B

Nombre _____

Fecha _____

Hora _____

Vocabulary Flash Cards, Sheet 1

Write the Spanish vocabulary word below each picture. If there is a word or phrase, copy it in the space provided. Be sure to include the article for each noun.

Realidades **A**

Capítulo 1B

Nombre _____

Hora _____

Fecha _____

Vocabulary Flash Cards, Sheet 2

_____

_____

_____

_____

_____

**bueno,
buena**

_____ ,

_____

**atrevido,
atrevida**

_____ ,

_____

paciente

_____

**reservado,
reservada**

_____ ,

_____

Realidades **A**

Capítulo 1B

Nombre _____

Fecha _____

Hora _____

Vocabulary Flash Cards, Sheet 3

simpático, simpática	talentoso, talentosa	yo
_____, _____	_____, _____	_____
él	ella	según mi familia
_____	_____	_____ _____
el amigo	la amiga	a veces
_____ _____	_____ _____	_____ _____

Realidades **A**

Capítulo 1B

Nombre _____

Hora _____

Fecha _____

Vocabulary Flash Cards, Sheet 4

muy	pero	según
_____	_____	_____
_____ _____	_____ _____	_____ _____
_____ _____	_____ _____	_____ _____

Tear out this page. Write the English words on the lines. Fold the paper along the dotted line to see the correct answers so you can check your work.

artístico, artística _____

atrevido, atrevida _____

bueno, buena _____

deportista _____

desordenado, desordenada _____

estudioso, estudiosa _____

gracioso, graciosa _____

impaciente _____

inteligente _____

ordenado, ordenada _____

paciente _____

perezoso, perezosa _____

Fold In

Realidades A

Capítulo 1B

Nombre _____

Hora _____

Fecha _____

Vocabulary Check, Sheet 2

Tear out this page. Write the Spanish words on the lines. Fold the paper along the dotted line to see the correct answers so you can check your work.

artistic _____

_____

daring _____

_____

good _____

sports-minded _____

messy _____

_____

studious _____

_____

funny _____

_____

impatient _____

intelligent _____

neat _____

_____

patient _____

lazy _____

_____

Fold In

Tear out this page. Write the English words on the lines. Fold the paper along the dotted line to see the correct answers so you can check your work.

reservado, reservada _____

serio, seria _____

simpático, simpática _____

sociable _____

talentoso, talentosa _____

trabajador, trabajadora _____

el chico _____

la chica _____

el amigo _____

la amiga _____

yo _____

él _____

ella _____

muy _____

según mi familia _____

_____

Fold In

Realidades A

Capítulo 1B

Nombre _____

Hora _____

Fecha _____

Vocabulary Check, Sheet 4

Tear out this page. Write the Spanish words on the lines. Fold the paper along the dotted line to see the correct answers so you can check your work.

reserved, shy _____

_____

serious _____

nice, friendly _____

_____

sociable _____

talented _____

_____

hardworking _____

_____

boy _____

girl _____

friend (male) _____

friend (female) _____

I _____

he _____

she _____

very _____

according to _____
my family

To hear a complete list of the vocabulary for this chapter, go to Disc 1, Track 3 on the Guided Practice Audio CD, or go to www.phschool.com and type in the Web Code jcd-0199. Then click on **Repaso del capítulo.**

Fold In

Adjectives (p. 64)

- Words that describe people and things are called adjectives.
- Most Spanish adjectives have two forms: masculine (ends in -**o** like **simpático**) and feminine (ends in -**a** like **estudiosa**).
- Masculine adjectives are used with masculine nouns: <u>Tomás</u> **es simpátic<u>o</u>**.
- Feminine adjectives are used with feminine nouns: <u>Luisa</u> **es estudios<u>a</u>**.
- Adjectives that end in -**e** and -**ista** may be used with either masculine or feminine nouns:

    <u>Tomás</u> **es inteligent<u>e</u>**. <u>Luisa</u> **es inteligent<u>e</u> también.**

    <u>Marcos</u> **es muy deport<u>ista</u>**. <u>Ana</u> **es muy deport<u>ista</u> también.**

- Adjectives with the masculine form -**dor** have -**dora** as the feminine form:

    <u>Juan</u> **es trabaja<u>dor</u>**. <u>Susana</u> **es trabaja<u>dora</u> también.**

A. Look at the adjectives below. Circle the ending of the adjective: -**o**, -**a**, -**or**, -**ora**, -**e**, or -**ista**.

1. trabajador
2. deportista
3. paciente

4. ordenada
5. inteligente
6. simpática

7. trabajadora
8. sociable
9. estudioso

B. Now, organize the adjectives from **part A** by writing them in the chart under the correct column heading. One has been done for you.

Masculine endings		Feminine endings		Masculine or feminine	
-o	-or	-a	-ora	-e	-ista
	trabajador				

C. Now look at the following sentences. Write **M** next to the sentences where the adjective is masculine. Write **F** next to the sentences where the adjective is feminine. Write **E** next to the sentences where the adjective could be *either* masculine or feminine.

_____ 1. Yo soy muy simpática.

_____ 2. Tú eres muy estudioso.

_____ 3. Tú eres muy ordenado.

_____ 4. Yo soy muy trabajadora.

_____ 5. Yo soy muy inteligente.

_____ 6. Tú eres muy trabajador.

_____ 7. Yo soy muy paciente.

_____ 8. Yo soy muy deportista.

_____ 9. Tú eres muy reservada.

_____ 10. Tú eres muy impaciente.

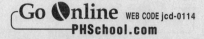
WEB CODE jcd-0114
PHSchool.com

Realidades (A)

Capítulo 1B

Nombre _____

Fecha _____

Hora _____

Guided Practice Activities 1B-2

Adjectives *(continued)*

D. Choose the correct adjective to complete each sentence and write it in the blank.

1.

Raúl es (**estudioso / estudiosa**) _____.

2.

Rebeca es (**artístico / artística**) _____.

3.

Pedro es muy (**ordenado / ordenada**) _____.

4.

Paulina es muy (**atrevido / atrevida**) _____.

5.

Javier es (**trabajador / trabajadora**) _____.

6.

Elena es (**perezoso / perezosa**) _____.

E. Now, choose the correct adjective in each sentence to describe yourself. Write the adjective in the blank.

1. Yo soy (**paciente / impaciente**) _____.

2. Soy (**simpático / simpática**) _____.

3. También soy (**trabajador / trabajadora**) _____.

4. No soy (**serio / seria**) _____.

Go Online WEB CODE jcd-0114
PHSchool.com

Realidades (A)

Capítulo 1B

Nombre _____

Hora _____

Fecha _____

Guided Practice Activities 1B-3

Definite and indefinite articles (p. 70)

- **El** and **la** are the Spanish *definite articles*. They mean the same as "the" in English.
- You use **el** with masculine nouns: **el libro**. You use **la** with feminine nouns: **la carpeta**.
- **Un** and **una** are the Spanish *indefinite articles*. They mean the same as "a" and "an" in English.
- You use **un** with masculine nouns: **un libro**. You use **una** with feminine nouns: **una carpeta**.

A. Look at the ending of each noun in this group. Decide if the noun is masculine or feminine. Write **M** next to the masculine words and **F** next to the feminine words. Follow the model.

| Modelo | __*F*__ computadora | | |

1. _____ año   3. _____ libro   5. _____ carpeta

2. _____ semana   4. _____ hoja   6. _____ profesor

B. Now, look at the words from **part A** again and circle the definite article **el** for the masculine words and the definite article **la** for the feminine words.

1. (el / la) año   3. (el / la) libro   5. (el / la) carpeta

2. (el / la) semana   4. (el / la) hoja   6. (el / la) profesor

C. Look at the ending of each noun below. Decide if the word is masculine or feminine. Write **M** next to the masculine words and **F** next to the feminine words.

1. _____ cuaderno   3. _____ revista   5. _____ bicicleta

2. _____ amigo   4. _____ familia   6. _____ cuento

D. Now, look at the words from **part C** again and circle the indefinite article **un** for the masculine words and the indefinite article **una** for the feminine words.

1. (un / una) cuaderno   3. (un / una) revista   5. (un / una) bicicleta

2. (un / una) amigo   4. (un / una) familia   6. (un / una) cuento

E. Circle the correct definite or indefinite article to complete each sentence.

1. (El / La) estudiante es estudiosa.   5. (El / La) profesor es trabajador.

2. (El / La) profesora es buena.   6. (Un / Una) estudiante es artístico.

3. (Un / Una) amigo es simpático.   7. (El / La) amiga es inteligente.

4. (Un / Una) estudiante es atrevida.   8. (Un / Una) estudiante es reservada.

Realidades Ⓐ

Capítulo 1B

Nombre _____

Fecha _____

Hora _____

Guided Practice Activities 1B-4

Word order: Placement of adjectives (p. 72)

- English adjectives usually come *before* the noun they describe.
- Spanish adjectives usually come *after* the noun they describe:

  Olga es una <u>chica talentosa</u>.

- Many Spanish sentences follow this pattern:

  <u>subject noun</u> + <u>verb</u> + <u>indefinite article and noun</u> + <u>adjective</u>

       1   2   3   4

  <u>Roberto</u> <u>es</u> <u>un estudiante</u> <u>bueno</u>.   **<u>Serena</u> <u>es</u> <u>una chica</u> <u>inteligente</u>.**
    1   2   3   4   1   2   3   4

A. Look at the following groups of words. Write a number from **1** to **4** below each word according to what kind of word it is. Follow the model and use the examples above.

- Write **1** for subject nouns.
- Write **2** for verbs.
- Write **3** for indefinite articles and nouns.
- Write **4** for adjectives.

Modelo	es / Diego / talentoso / un estudiante
	2 1 4 3

1. seria / Olga / una estudiante / es

2. un amigo / es / bueno / Guillermo

3. Javier / un estudiante / es / trabajador

4. es / Concha / simpática / una chica

5. es / una estudiante / Ana / inteligente

6. Manuel / es / atrevido / un chico

B. Now, write the complete sentence for each example from **part A** by putting the words in order by the numbers you added, going from 1 to 4. Follow the model.

Modelo	*Diego es un estudiante talentoso.*

1. _____

2. _____

3. _____

4. _____

5. _____

6. _____

Go Online WEB CODE jcd-0115
PHSchool.com

Realidades Ⓐ

Capítulo 1B

Nombre _____

Hora _____

Fecha _____

Guided Practice Activities 1B-5

Lectura: Un *self-quiz* (pp. 76–77)

A. You have seen many cognates used in your textbook. Cognates are related words in different languages; for example, the word **profesor** in Spanish is a *professor* or *teacher* in English. Cognates occur in your vocabulary lists and in readings. Look at the cognates below and write the English word for each on the line provided. Follow the model.

Modelo   bicicleta   <u>*bicycle*</u>

1. computadora _____

2. básquetbol _____

3. la tele _____

4. los colores _____

5. verbo _____

6. usar _____

7. organizar _____

8. estudiar _____

B. Now, read the following section from your textbook. You will find even more cognates in this reading. Find the Spanish word that corresponds to each English word below. Write the Spanish word on the lines provided.

> *¡Los colores revelan tu personalidad!*
> *¿Eres una chica? ¿Te gusta el verde? Eres una chica natural.*
> *¿Eres una chica? ¿Te gusta el azul? Eres muy talentosa.*
> *¿Eres una chica? ¿Te gusta el violeta? Eres muy independiente.*

• personality _____

• natural _____

• talented _____

• independent _____

• violet _____

C. The reading in your textbook is a self-quiz that tells you information about your personality based on the colors you like and whether you are a boy or a girl. Based on the information given below and what you learned from the reading, circle if you are a boy or a girl. Then, write what color you like. Follow the model.

Modelo   Eres romántico. Eres ((un chico) / una chica). Te gusta ____*el violeta*____.

1. Eres atrevido. Eres (**un chico** / **una chica**). Te gusta _____.

2. Eres muy talentosa. Eres (**un chico** / **una chica**). Te gusta _____.

3. Eres artística. Eres (**un chico** / **una chica**). Te gusta _____.

Go Online WEB CODE jcd-0116
PHSchool.com

Realidades A

Capítulo 1B

Nombre _____

Hora _____

Fecha _____

Guided Practice Activities 1B-6

Presentación escrita (p. 79)

Task: Write an e-mail in which you introduce yourself to a prospective pen pal.

❶ Prewrite. In order to introduce yourself to a new friend, you need to first organize what you are going to include. Fill in the form below with your personal information.

Me llamo _____ .

Soy (*use adjectives to describe yourself*) _____

_____ .

Me gusta _____ .

No me gusta _____ .

❷ Draft. Read the following e-mail that another student has written. You should use this to guide you in drafting your own e-mail.

> *¡Hola! Me llamo Pilar. Soy una chica artística y muy independiente. Me gusta mucho dibujar y usar la computadora, pero me gusta más bailar. Me gusta la música salsa. No me gusta nada practicar deportes. ¿Cómo eres tú? Escríbeme pronto.*

Now, create an e-mail similar to the one above writing in your information from **part 1**.

¡Hola! Me llamo _____ . Soy (**un chico** / **una chica**) _____

_____ y _____ . Me gusta mucho _____

_____ , pero me gusta más _____ .

Me gusta _____ . No me gusta _____ .

¿Cómo eres tú? Escríbeme pronto.

❸ Revise. Exchange papers with another student in your class. Use the following checklist to review your partner's e-mail and also when you rewrite yours. If you need help figuring out what is correct, use the model from the **Prewrite** section above.

_____ Is there enough information provided for each question in the prewrite stage?
- stated his/her name
- described himself/herself
- said what he/she likes to do
- said what he/she doesn't like to do

_____ Is the spelling correct? (Use a dictionary if you are not sure.)

_____ Are the adjectives in the correct form? (Think, is the student male or female?)

_____ Is there an opening and a closing?

❹ Publish. Write your revised e-mail on a separate sheet of paper. Your teacher may ask you to type the e-mail and send it to a prospective pen pal.

Realidades (A)

Capítulo 2A

Nombre _____

Hora _____

Fecha _____

Vocabulary Flash Cards, Sheet 1

Write the Spanish vocabulary word below each picture. If there is a word or phrase, copy it in the space provided. Be sure to include the article for each noun.

Horario	
Hora	**Clase**
Primera hora	inglés
Segunda hora	matemáticas
Tercera hora	arte
Cuarta hora	ciencias sociales
Quinta hora	el almuerzo
Sexta hora	tecnología
Séptima hora	español
Octava hora	educación física
Novena hora	ciencas naturales

Realidades Ⓐ

Capítulo 2A

Nombre _____

Hora _____

Fecha _____

Vocabulary Flash Cards, Sheet 2

_____

_____

_____

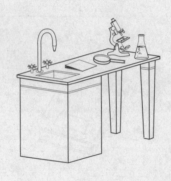

_____

_____

la clase

_____

hablar

_____

necesito

_____

en la ... hora	**primero, primera**	**segundo, segunda**
_____ _____ _____	_____, _____	_____, _____
tercero, tercera	**cuarto, cuarta**	**quinto, quinta**
_____, _____	_____, _____	_____, _____
sexto, sexta	**séptimo, séptima**	**octavo, octava**
_____, _____	_____, _____	_____, _____

Realidades Ⓐ

Capítulo 2A

Nombre _____

Hora _____

Fecha _____

Vocabulary Flash Cards, Sheet 4

**noveno,
novena**

_____,

_____

**décimo,
décima**

_____,

_____

**aburrido,
aburrida**

_____,

_____

difícil

_____

**divertido,
divertida**

_____,

fácil

_____

**favorito,
favorita**

_____,

_____

interesante

_____

**práctico,
práctica**

_____,

_____

Realidades A

Capítulo 2A

Nombre _____

Hora _____

Fecha _____

Vocabulary Flash Cards, Sheet 5

más...que

_____

_____

a ver...

_____

_____

¿Quién?

_____

para

_____

mucho

_____

la
tarea

_____

_____

la
clase de ...

_____

_____

necesitas

_____

(yo)
tengo

_____

_____

Realidades Ⓐ

Capítulo 2A

Nombre _____

Hora _____

Fecha _____

Vocabulary Flash Cards, Sheet 6

(tú)
tienes

_____

_____

_____

_____

_____

_____

_____

_____

_____

_____

_____

_____

_____

_____

_____

_____

_____

_____

Realidades A

Capítulo 2A

Nombre _____

Hora _____

Fecha _____

Vocabulary Check, Sheet 1

Tear out this page. Write the English words on the lines. Fold the paper along the dotted line to see the correct answers so you can check your work.

el almuerzo   _____

la clase   _____

arte   _____

español   _____

ciencias naturales   _____

ciencias sociales   _____

educación física   _____

inglés   _____

matemáticas   _____

tecnología   _____

el horario   _____

la tarea   _____

enseñar   _____

estudiar   _____

hablar   _____

primero, primera   _____

segundo, segunda   _____

Fold In

Realidades Ⓐ

Capítulo 2A

Nombre _____

Fecha _____

Hora _____

Vocabulary Check, Sheet 2

Tear out this page. Write the Spanish words on the lines. Fold the paper along the dotted line to see the correct answers so you can check your work.

lunch _____

class _____

art _____

Spanish _____

science _____

social studies _____

physical education _____

English _____

mathematics _____

technology/ computers _____

schedule _____

homework _____

to teach _____

to study _____

to talk _____

first _____

second _____

Fold In ←

Tear out this page. Write the English words on the lines. Fold the paper along the dotted line to see the correct answers so you can check your work.

tercer, tercero, tercera _____

cuarto, cuarta _____

quinto, quinta _____

sexto, sexta _____

séptimo, séptima _____

octavo, octava _____

noveno, novena _____

décimo, décima _____

la calculadora _____

la carpeta de argollas _____
_____

el diccionario _____

aburrido, aburrida _____

difícil _____

fácil _____

Fold In

Tear out this page. Write the Spanish words on the lines. Fold the paper along the dotted line to see the correct answers so you can check your work.

third _____

fourth _____

fifth _____

sixth _____

seventh _____

eighth _____

ninth _____

tenth _____

calculator _____

three-ring
binder _____

_____

dictionary _____

boring _____

difficult _____

easy _____

To hear a complete list of the vocabulary for this chapter, go to Disc 1, Track 4 on the Guided Practice Audio CD, or go to www.phschool.com and type in the Web Code jcd-0289. Then click on **Repaso del capítulo.**

Fold In

Realidades Ⓐ

Capítulo 2A

Nombre _____

Hora _____

Fecha _____

Guided Practice Activities 2A-1

Subject pronouns (p. 98)

- The subject of the sentence tells who is doing the action. It is often a name:
  <u>Ana</u> **canta.**

- Subject pronouns replace people's names to say who is doing an action:
  <u>Ella</u> **canta.** <u>Tú</u> **bailas.**

- Here are the Spanish subject pronouns:

Singular	Plural
yo (I)	**nosotros** (we, *masculine or mixed*)
tú (you, *familiar*)	**nosotras** (we, *feminine*)
usted (you, *formal*)	**vosotros** (you, *familiar plural, masculine or mixed*)
él (he)	**vosotras** (you, *familiar plural, feminine*)
ella (she)	**ustedes** (you, *formal plural*)
	ellos (they, *masculine or mixed*)
	ellas (they, *feminine*)

- **Vosotros** and **vosotras** are primarily used in Spain.

- **Usted** and **ustedes** are formal forms that are used with people you address with a title, such as **señor** and **doctor**.

- In Latin America, **ustedes** is also used when addressing two or more people you call **tú** individually.

A. Write the twelve subject pronouns listed above in the correct category of the chart. Follow the model.

Singular			Plural		
Masculine only	**Feminine only**	**Masculine or feminine**	**Masculine or mixed**	**Feminine only**	**Masculine or feminine**
él					

B. Look at the English subject pronouns below. Use the list above to help you circle the Spanish subject pronoun that corresponds to the English pronoun.

1. *I* (**él** / **yo**)
2. *we* (**nosotros** / **vosotros**)
3. *you* (**ella** / **usted**)
4. *they* (**ellos** / **ustedes**)
5. *he* (**tú** / **él**)

6. *we* (**usted** / **nosotras**)
7. *you* (**nosotras** / **tú**)
8. *you* (**ellas** / **ustedes**)
9. *she* (**él** / **ella**)
10. *they* (**nosotras** / **ellas**)

Subject pronouns *(continued)*

C. Circle the subject pronoun that is best associated with each group of names.

1. Susana, Luisa, Marta: (**ellos** / **ellas**)

2. Pablo: (**él** / **ella**)

3. el señor Rivas: (**tú** / **usted**)

4. la señora Rivas: (**tú** / **usted**)

5. Alberto y tú: (**ustedes** / **nosotros**)

6. Sandra y ella: (**ellos** / **ellas**)

7. Marcos y María: (**ellos** / **ellas**)

8. el señor Rodríguez y la señora Rodríguez: (**ustedes** / **vosotros**)

9. Teresa: (**él** / **ella**)

10. Martín y Roberto: (**ellos** / **ellas**)

D. Look at the following drawings and answer the questions using subject pronouns. Follow the model.

Modelo ¿Quién es?

Es _____él_____ .

1. ¿Quién es?

Es _____ .

4. ¿Quién soy?

Soy _____ .

2. ¿Quiénes son?

Son _____ .

5. ¿Quiénes son?

Somos _____ .

3. ¿Quién es?

Es _____ .

Go Online WEB CODE jcd-0203
PHSchool.com

Realidades Ⓐ

Capítulo 2A

Nombre _____

Hora _____

Fecha _____

Guided Practice Activities 2A-3

Present tense of -ar verbs (p. 100)

- An infinitive is the most basic form of a verb. In English, infinitives have the word "to" in front of them (to talk). In Spanish, infinitives end in **-ar**, **-er**, or **-ir**.
- The largest number of Spanish infinitives end in **-ar**: **hablar, cantar,** etc.
- To create the present tense of most of these verbs, drop the **-ar** from the stem: **habl-, cant-,** etc.
- Add the verb endings:

yo: add **-o**: **hablo**	nosotros/nosotras: add **-amos**: hablamos
tú: add **-as**: **hablas**	vosotros/vosotras: add **-áis**: habláis
usted/él/ella: add **-a**: **habla**	ustedes/ellos/ellas: add **-an**: hablan

A. Look at each verb form. Circle the ending. Follow the model.

Modelo   estudiⓐ

1. hablas
2. nado
3. canta
4. tocamos
5. trabajas

6. patinamos
7. dibujan
8. bailo
9. pasan
10. escucha

B. Now, look at the same list of verb forms from **part A** and circle the subject pronoun that matches each verb.

1. (**usted** / **tú**) hablas
2. (**yo** / **ella**) nado
3. (**usted** / **yo**) canta
4. (**nosotros** / **vosotros**) tocamos
5. (**tú** / **usted**) trabajas

6. (**ellos** / **nosotras**) patinamos
7. (**ustedes** / **nosotros**) dibujan
8. (**yo** / **él**) bailo
9. (**ellas** / **usted**) pasan
10. (**ella** / **ustedes**) escucha

Realidades Ⓐ

Capítulo 2A

Nombre _____

Hora _____

Fecha _____

Guided Practice Activities 2A-4

Present tense of -ar verbs (continued)

C. Complete each sentence by writing the correct **-ar** verb ending on the line provided. Follow the model.

Modelo   Ellas mont_an_ en bicicleta.

1. Marta trabaj_____ .

2. Yo cant_____.

3. Tú esquí_____.

4. Ellos patin_____.

5. Nosotros bail_____.

D. Now, complete each sentence with the correct verb form of the infinitive in parentheses. Follow the model.

Modelo   Tú (nadar) _____nada_s_____.

1. Yo (bailar) _____.

2. Ella (cantar) _____.

3. Nosotros (trabajar) _____.

4. Ustedes (patinar) _____.

5. Ellos (esquiar) _____.

6. Tú (nadar) _____.

7. Él (dibujar) _____.

8. Ellas (usar) _____ la computadora.

E. Create complete sentences using the subject pronoun provided. Follow the model.

Modelo   tú /   _Tú dibujas._

1. él /

_____

2. nosotros /

_____

3. ellos /

_____

4. yo /

_____

Go Online WEB CODE jcd-0204
PHSchool.com

Realidades A

Capítulo 2A

Nombre _____

Hora _____

Fecha _____

Guided Practice Activities 2A-5

Lectura: La Escuela Español Vivo (pp. 108–109)

A. The reading in your textbook is a brochure for a school called **Español Vivo**. The following is an excerpt from that reading. Read and answer the questions that follow.

❙❙ *Es verano, el mes de junio. Eres estudiante en Santa Ana, un pueblo en las montañas de Costa Rica.* ❙❙

1. Underline the season and month in the paragraph above.
2. Circle the town and country where the school is located.
3. What does the word **montañas** mean? _____

B. Here is another excerpt from that same reading. Read and answer the questions below.

❙❙ *Hay cinco estudiantes en tu clase. Uds. escuchan, hablan y practican el español todo el día. También usan la computadora.* ❙❙

1. How many students are in the class? _____
2. Circle the four activities from the reading that students do in class (just circle the verbs).
3. How many of the verbs that you circled in number 2 go with the word **el español**?
   _____ Which ones? _____

C. Look at the reading on the top of the second page in your textbook.

1. Circle the one activity listed below that is NOT something you can do on the weekends in Costa Rica.
   a. visitar un volcán
   b. visitar un parque nacional
   c. nadar en el mar Mediterráneo
   d. nadar en el océano Pacífico

2. There are many cognates in the four examples above. Write the Spanish word or words, choosing from examples **a** through **d**, that go with the English words below.
   - visit _____
   - volcano _____
   - national park _____
   - Mediterranean _____
   - Pacific Ocean _____

D. Look at the schedule for the school day in the **Español Vivo** school. Answer the questions that follow.

Hora	lunes a viernes
08:00–10:30	Clases de español
10:30–11:00	Recreo
11:00–13:00	Clases de español
13:00–14:00	Almuerzo
14:00–15:30	Conversaciones
15:30–16:30	Clase de música y baile

1. At what times do the students go to classes?
   at _____, _____, and _____
2. When do students have conversations? at _____
3. Since there is no A.M. or P.M., how do you know when the clock goes over to afternoon hours? _____

Presentación oral (p. 111)

Task: Imagine that a student from Costa Rica has just arrived at your school. Tell the student about some of your classes.

A. Fill in the chart below with information on three of your classes. Follow the model.

Hora	Clase	Comentarios	Profesor(a)
primera	la clase de arte	me gusta dibujar	el Sr. Gómez

B. Before writing up your own presentation, read the following sample. Read it out loud the second time through to get an idea of how long it will take you to do your presentation.

‖ *En la primera hora tengo la clase de arte. Me gusta dibujar. La clase es mi favorita. El Sr. Gómez es el profesor.* ‖

When speaking, remember to do the following:

_____ speak clearly

_____ use complete sentences

_____ read all information

C. Now, fill in the paragraph below with information about one of your classes.

En la _____ hora tengo la clase de _____.

Me gusta _____. La clase es _____.

_____ es el (la) profesor(a).

D. When the teacher asks you to present your work, you will describe the one class as you see it in **part C.** Your teacher will be grading you on:

- how complete your preparation is
- how much information you communicate
- how easy it is to understand you.

Realidades Ⓐ

Capítulo 2B

Nombre _____

Hora _____

Fecha _____

Vocabulary Flash Cards, Sheet 1

Write the Spanish vocabulary word below each picture. If there is a word or phrase, copy it in the space provided. Be sure to include the article for each noun.

Realidades **A**

Capítulo 2B

Nombre _____

Hora _____

Fecha _____

Vocabulary Flash Cards, Sheet 2

de

Hay

Realidades Ⓐ

Capítulo 2B

Nombre _____

Hora _____

Fecha _____

Vocabulary Flash Cards, Sheet 3

al lado de	detrás de	allí
_____ _____ _____	_____	_____

debajo de	encima de	aquí
_____ _____	_____ _____	_____

delante de	en	¿Dónde?
_____ _____	_____	_____

Realidades **A**

Capítulo 2B

mi	**tu**	**Es un(a)...**
_____	_____	_____
¿Qué es esto?	**los, las**	**unos, unas**
_____	_____	_____
_____	_____	_____
_____	_____	_____
_____	_____	_____

Nombre _____

Hora _____

Fecha _____

Vocabulary Check, Sheet 1

Tear out this page. Write the English words on the lines. Fold the paper along the dotted line to see the correct answers so you can check your work.

la bandera _____

el cartel _____

la computadora _____

el disquete _____

la mochila _____

_____

la pantalla _____

la papelera _____

_____

el ratón _____

el reloj _____

el sacapuntas _____

_____

el teclado _____

el escritorio _____

la mesa _____

la silla _____

la puerta _____

Fold In

Tear out this page. Write the Spanish words on the lines. Fold the paper along
the dotted line to see the correct answers so you can check your work.

flag _____

poster _____

computer _____

diskette _____

bookbag,
backpack _____

(computer) screen _____

wastepaper
basket _____

(computer) mouse _____

clock _____

pencil
sharpener _____

(computer) keyboard _____

desk _____

table _____

chair _____

door _____

Fold In

Tear out this page. Write the English words on the lines. Fold the paper along the dotted line to see the correct answers so you can check your work.

la ventana _____

al lado de _____

allí _____

aquí _____

debajo de _____

delante de _____

detrás de _____

¿Dónde? _____

en _____

encima de _____

Hay _____

Fold In ←

Tear out this page. Write the Spanish words on the lines. Fold the paper along the dotted line to see the correct answers so you can check your work.

window _____

next to _____

there _____

here _____

underneath _____

in front of _____

behind _____

Where? _____

in, on _____

on top of _____

There is, There are _____

Fold In

To hear a complete list of the vocabulary for this chapter, go to Disc 1, Track 5 on the Guided Practice Audio CD, or go to www.phschool.com and type in the Web Code jcd-0299. Then click on **Repaso del capítulo.**

Realidades A

Capítulo 2B

Nombre _____

Fecha _____

Hora _____

Guided Practice Activities 2B-1

The verb *estar* (p. 128)

- Irregular verbs do not follow the same pattern as regular verbs.
- **Estar** (*to be*) is irregular. Its **yo** form (**estoy**) is different from the regular **-ar yo** form. Its **tú**, **usted/él/ella**, and **ustedes/ellos/ellas** forms are different because they have an accent on the **a**: **estás, está, están**.
- Here are the forms of **estar**:

yo	**estoy**	nosotros/nosotras	**estamos**
tú	**estás**	vosotros/vosotras	**estáis**
usted/él/ella	**está**	ustedes/ellos/ellas	**están**

- **Estar** is used to tell how someone feels or to give a location.

A. Circle the ending of each form of **estar**.

1. yo estoy
2. tú estás
3. Ud. está

4. nosotras estamos
5. ellos están

B. Now, complete each sentence by writing in the correct ending for the correct form of **estar**.

1. Tú est_____ en la clase de arte.
2. Ellos est_____ en la clase de ciencias.
3. Nosotros est_____ en la clase de español.
4. Yo est_____ en la clase de matemáticas.
5. Él est_____ en la clase de literatura.
6. Usted est_____ en la oficina.
7. Ustedes est_____ en la sala de clase.
8. Nosotras est_____ en la clase de tecnología.

C. Complete each sentence with the correct form of **estar**.

1. Yo _____ bien.
2. Tú _____ muy bien.
3. Ella _____ regular.
4. Nosotras _____ bien.

5. Usted _____ regular.
6. Ellos _____ bien.
7. Él _____ regular.
8. Ustedes _____ bien.

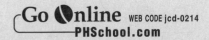

The verb *estar* (continued)

D. Complete the conversation with correct forms of **estar**.

LUISA: ¡Buenos días! ¿Cómo _____ ustedes?

ANA E INÉS: Nosotras _____ bien. ¿Y tú? ¿Cómo _____?

LUISA: Yo _____ muy bien. ¿Dónde _____ Marcos y Marta?

ANA: Marcos _____ en la clase de español. Marta _____ en la clase de matemáticas.

E. Create complete sentences with **estar**. Follow the model.

Modelo usted / estar / en la clase de matemáticas

    Usted está en la clase de matemáticas _____.

1. tú / estar / en la clase de español

    _____.

2. ellas / estar / en la clase de arte

    _____.

3. nosotros / estar / en la clase de inglés

    _____.

4. usted / estar / en la clase de matemáticas

    _____.

5. yo / estar / en la clase de tecnología

    _____.

6. él / estar / en la clase de ciencias sociales

    _____.

Go Online WEB CODE jcd-0214
PHSchool.com

The plurals of nouns and articles (p. 132)

Plural of nouns		Plural definite articles		Plural indefinite articles	
Ends in vowel	Ends in consonant	Masculine	Feminine	Masculine	Feminine
add -s: libros, sillas	add -es: relojes, carteles	los (*the*) los libros	las (*the*) las sillas	unos (*some, a few*) unos libros	unas (*some, a few*) unas sillas

● Nouns that end in -z change the z to c in the plural: **lápiz** → **lápices**.

A. Circle the ending of each noun. Is it a vowel or a consonant? Write **V** for vowel or **C** for consonant next to each word.

1. _____ cartel
2. _____ teclado
3. _____ mochila
4. _____ mes

5. _____ bandera
6. _____ reloj
7. _____ disquete
8. _____ profesor

B. Now, look at the same words from **part A** and add the endings to make them plural.

1. cartel_____
2. teclado_____
3. mochila_____
4. mes_____

5. bandera_____
6. reloj_____
7. disquete_____
8. profesor_____

C. Now, write the *complete* plural form of each word from **part B**.

1. cartel   _____
2. teclado   _____
3. mochila   _____
4. mes   _____
5. bandera   _____
6. reloj   _____
7. disquete   _____
8. profesor   _____

The plurals of nouns and articles (*continued*)

D. Identify whether each of the words from **part C** are masculine or feminine. Write **M** for masculine or **F** for feminine next to each word.

1. _____ cartel

2. _____ teclado

3. _____ mochila

4. _____ mes

5. _____ bandera

6. _____ reloj

7. _____ disquete

8. _____ profesor

E. Now, look at the words from **part D** in the plural. Circle the correct definite article, masculine or feminine.

1. (los / las) carteles

2. (los / las) teclados

3. (los / las) mochilas

4. (los / las) meses

5. (los / las) banderas

6. (los / las) relojes

7. (los / las) disquetes

8. (los / las) profesores

F. Look at each noun below and write **los** or **las**, depending on whether the word is masculine or feminine.

1. _____ puertas

2. _____ ventanas

3. _____ horarios

4. _____ lápices

5. _____ ratones

6. _____ pantallas

G. Look at the words from **part E** again. This time, circle the correct indefinite article, masculine or feminine.

1. (unos / unas) carteles

2. (unos / unas) teclados

3. (unos / unas) mochilas

4. (unos / unas) meses

5. (unos / unas) banderas

6. (unos / unas) relojes

7. (unos / unas) disquetes

8. (unos / unas) profesores

H. Look at the nouns from **part F** again. Now, write **unos** or **unas**, depending on whether the word is masculine or feminine.

1. _____ puertas

2. _____ ventanas

3. _____ horarios

4. _____ lápices

5. _____ ratones

6. _____ pantallas

Lectura: El UNICEF y una convención para los niños (pp. 138–139)

A. The reading in your textbook talks about the organization UNICEF (United Nations International Children's Emergency Fund). You will see many cognates in the reading. Look through the reading and find the Spanish words that most closely resemble the ones below. Write the words in the spaces provided.

1. convention _____
2. dignity _____
3. nations _____
4. protection _____
5. special _____

6. diet _____
7. opinions _____
8. community _____
9. violence _____
10. privilege _____

B. Look at the first paragraph from the reading in your textbook. Write down three things that are said to be privileges for children.

1. _____
2. _____
3. _____

C. Read the following excerpt from your textbook and answer the questions that follow.

❚❚ *UNICEF...tiene siete oficinas regionales en diversas naciones y un Centro de Investigaciones en Italia.* ❚❚

1. Where does UNICEF have seven regional offices?

_____

2. Where is there a Center of Investigation for UNICEF?

_____

D. Look again at the bulleted list in your textbook and list five things in the spaces below that the convention said that all children need.

1. _____
2. _____
3. _____
4. _____
5. _____

Presentación escrita (p. 141)

Task: Pretend you have a pen pal from Mexico who is coming to visit your school next semester. Write your pen pal a note describing your Spanish classroom.

❶ Prewrite.

A. On a separate sheet of paper draw a sketch of your Spanish classroom. You will use this as a reference when writing your note. Try to include four or five different items.

B. Label the items in your sketch using words from your vocabulary.

❷ Draft.

A. Read the sample note written by another student. Use this to guide your own writing.

> *En mi sala de clases hay cinco ventanas. Mi pupitre está al lado del escritorio del profesor. La puerta está detrás de mi pupitre. Hay una bandera encima de la mesa de computadoras.*

B. Look at the sample note again and list, in the spaces below, all of the classroom objects mentioned.

_____   _____   _____

_____   _____   _____

C. Compare the list of words in **part B** with the words you labeled in your sketch. This will help you get an idea of how similar your draft will be to the model. Create three sentences below filling in what items are in your classroom and where they are located.

1. Hay _____.

2. _____ está _____.

3. _____ está _____.

❸ Revise. Read through your draft to see if it makes sense to you. Share your work with a partner who should check the following:

_____ Are the sentences easy to understand?

_____ Did you leave out anything from your drawing?

_____ Are there any spelling or grammar errors?

_____ If there are any problems with your draft, make a revised draft.

Realidades A

Capítulo 3A

Nombre _____

Hora _____

Fecha _____

Vocabulary Flash Cards, Sheet 1

Write the Spanish vocabulary word below each picture. If there is a word or phrase, copy it in the space provided. Be sure to include the article for each noun.

_____	_____	_____
_____	_____	_____
_____	_____	_____

_____

_____

_____

_____

_____

_____

_____

_____

_____

_____

_____

_____

_____

_____

Realidades Ⓐ

Capítulo 3A

Nombre _____

Hora _____

Fecha _____

Vocabulary Flash Cards, Sheet 3

_____

_____

_____

_____

_____

_____

_____

_____

_____

_____

_____

_____

_____

_____

_____

Realidades **A**

Capítulo 3A

Nombre _____

Hora _____

Fecha _____

Vocabulary Flash Cards, Sheet 4

la manzana _____ _____	**la ensalada** _____ _____	**en el almuerzo** _____ _____ _____
las fresas _____ _____	**en el desayuno** _____ _____ _____	**el pan** _____ _____ _____
el desayuno _____ _____	**la comida** _____ _____	**beber** _____ _____

beber _____	**comer** _____	**compartir** _____
nunca _____	**siempre** _____	**todos los días** _____ _____ _____
por supuesto _____ _____	**¡Qué asco!** _____ _____	**¿Verdad?** _____ _____

Realidades **A**

Capítulo 3A

Nombre _____

Hora _____

Fecha _____

Vocabulary Flash Cards, Sheet 6

con _____	**¿Cuál?** _____	**más o menos** _____ _____
sin _____	**Me encanta(n) ...** _____	**Te encanta(s) ...** _____
Me gusta(n) ... _____ _____	**Te gusta(n) ...** _____ _____	

Nombre _____

Hora _____

Fecha _____

Tear out this page. Write the English words on the lines. Fold the paper along the dotted line to see the correct answers so you can check your work.

en el desayuno _____

los huevos _____

el pan _____

el pan tostado _____

el plátano _____

la salchicha _____

el tocino _____

el yogur _____

en el almuerzo _____

la ensalada
de frutas _____

las fresas _____

la galleta _____

la hamburguesa _____

el jamón _____

las papas fritas _____

el perrito caliente _____

la pizza _____

Fold In

Realidades Ⓐ

Capítulo 3A

Nombre _____

Fecha _____

Hora _____

Vocabulary Check, Sheet 2

Tear out this page. Write the Spanish words on the lines. Fold the paper along the dotted line to see the correct answers so you can check your work.

for breakfast _____

eggs _____

bread _____

toast _____

banana _____

sausage _____

bacon _____

yogurt _____

for lunch _____

fruit salad _____

_____

strawberries _____

cookie _____

hamburger _____

ham _____

French fries _____

hot dog _____

pizza _____

Fold In ←

Realidades **A**

Capítulo 3A

Nombre _____

Hora _____

Fecha _____

Vocabulary Check, Sheet 3

Tear out this page. Write the English words on the lines. Fold the paper along the dotted line to see the correct answers so you can check your work.

el sándwich de jamón y queso _____ _____

la sopa de verduras _____

el agua _____

el café _____

el jugo de manzana _____

el jugo de naranja _____

la leche _____

la limonada _____

el refresco _____

el té helado _____

beber _____

comer _____

la comida _____

compartir _____

nunca _____

siempre _____

todos los días _____

Fold In

Realidades Ⓐ

Capítulo 3A

Nombre _____

Hora _____

Fecha _____

Vocabulary Check, Sheet 4

Tear out this page. Write the Spanish words on the lines. Fold the paper along the dotted line to see the correct answers so you can check your work.

ham and cheese _____
sandwich _____

vegetable soup _____
_____

water _____

coffee _____

apple juice _____

orange juice _____

milk _____

lemonade _____

soft drink _____

iced tea _____

to drink _____

to eat _____

food, meal _____

to share _____

never _____

always _____

every day _____

Fold In

To hear a complete list of the vocabulary for this chapter, go to Disc 1, Track 6 on the Guided Practice Audio CD, or go to www.phschool.com and type in the Web Code jcd-0389. Then click on **Repaso del capítulo**.

Present tense of -er and -ir verbs (p. 160)

- Like the **-ar** verbs you learned previously, regular **-er** and **-ir** verbs follow a similar pattern in the present tense.

- For **-er** and **-ir** verbs, drop the **-er** or **-ir** from the infinitive (**comer, escribir**, etc.) and add the appropriate endings. The endings are the same for **-er** and **-ir** verbs except for in the **nosotros** and **vosotros** forms.

Present tense of -er verbs: comer	
yo: add **-o: como**	nosotros/nosotras: add **-emos: comemos**
tú: add **-es: comes**	vosotros/vosotras: add **-éis: coméis**
usted/él/ella: add **-e: come**	ustedes/ellos/ellas: add **-en: comen**

Present tense of -ir verbs: escribir	
yo: add **-o: escribo**	nosotros/nosotras: add **-imos: escribimos**
tú: add **-es: escribes**	vosotros/vosotras: add **-ís: escribís**
usted/él/ella: add **-e: escribe**	ustedes/ellos/ellas: add **-en: escriben**

A. Circle the ending in each verb form below.

1. escribimos
2. comparten
3. bebes
4. corre
5. ven

6. leo
7. escribes
8. comprendemos
9. comparto
10. ve

B. Now, look at the list of verbs in **part A**. Circle the correct subject pronoun for each verb.

1. (**ustedes / nosotros**) escribimos
2. (**ustedes / ella**) comparten
3. (**nosotros / tú**) bebes
4. (**yo / ella**) corre
5. (**ellos / nosotros**) ven

6. (**yo / él**) leo
7. (**usted / tú**) escribes
8. (**nosotras / ellos**) comprendemos
9. (**usted / yo**) comparto
10. (**usted / ustedes**) ve

Realidades Ⓐ

Capítulo 3A

Nombre _____

Hora _____

Fecha _____

Guided Practice Activities 3A-2

Present tense of -er and -ir verbs (continued)

C. Complete each sentence by writing the correct **-er** verb ending for each word.

1. Yo beb_____ agua.

2. Nosotras corr_____.

3. Ella comprend_____ todo.

4. Tú le_____ una revista.

5. Ustedes com_____.

6. Nosotros le_____ unos libros.

D. Now, complete each sentence by writing the correct **-ir** verb ending.

1. Tú escrib_____ una carta.

2. Él compart_____ la comida.

3. Ellas escrib_____ cuentos.

4. Nosotros escrib_____ poemas.

5. Yo compart_____.

6. Nosotras compart_____.

E. Complete each sentence with the correct verb form of the infinitive in parentheses. Follow the models.

| Modelo | Tú (escribir) ____escribes____ . |
| | Ella (comer)_____come_____ . |

1. Yo (leer) _____ .

2. Ella (escribir) _____ .

3. Nosotros (ver) _____ .

4. Tú (compartir) _____ .

5. Nosotros (escribir) _____ .

6. Ellos (beber) _____ .

7. Usted (compartir) _____ .

8. Ellas (leer) _____ .

F. Now, write complete sentences using the words provided. Follow the model.

| Modelo | tú / ver / la / tele |
| | _Tú ves la tele._ |

1. yo / leer / una / revista

_____ .

2. tú / compartir / el / cuarto

_____ .

3. ellos / beber / té / helado

_____ .

4. nosotros / comer / papas fritas

_____ .

5. ella / escribir / una / carta

_____ .

6. nosotros / compartir / la / comida

_____ .

7. usted / correr / 10 kilómetros

_____ .

8. ustedes / escribir / cuentos

_____ .

Go Online WEB CODE jcd-0303
PHSchool.com

Me gustan, me encantan (p. 164)

- To say you like one thing, use **me gusta** (*I like*) or **me encanta** (*I love*).
- To say you like more than one thing, use **me gustan** or **me encantan**.
- Put **no** in front of **me gusta** or **me gustan** to say you don't like one or more things:

  No me gusta el café. No me gustan los huevos.

One thing (singular)	More than one thing (plural)
Me **gusta la leche.**	Me **gustan las manzanas.**
Me **encanta el té.**	Me **encantan los jugos.**

A. Look at each noun. Write **S** if the noun is singular. Write **P** if it is plural.

1. _____ el cereal   **5.** _____ las salchichas

2. _____ el tocino   **6.** _____ las papas

3. _____ los huevos   **7.** _____ el pan

4. _____ las manzanas   **8.** _____ la pizza

B. Now, look at sentences using the same nouns from **part A**. Complete the verbs by writing **a** for the singular nouns and **an** for the plural nouns. Follow the models.

Modelos   Me encant *a*____ el café.

             Me encant*an*____ las fresas.

1. Me gust_____ el cereal.   **5.** Me encant_____ las salchichas.

2. Me gust_____ el tocino.   **6.** Me gust_____ las papas.

3. Me encant_____ los huevos.   **7.** Me encant_____ el pan.

4. Me gust_____ las manzanas.   **8.** Me gust_____ la pizza.

C. Complete the following exchanges by circling the correct word in parenthesis.

1. ELENA: ¿Te (**gusta** / **gustan**) el helado?

     ENRIQUE: ¡Sí! Me (**encanta** / **encantan**) el helado.

2. BERTA: No me (**gusta** / **gustan**) las fresas.

     ANA: ¿No? ¡Me (**encanta** / **encantan**) las fresas!

3. JOSÉ: Me (**encanta** / **encantan**) la pizza.

     LUIS: ¿Sí? A mí no. ¡Pero me (**encanta** / **encantan**) las hamburguesas!

Realidades **A**

Capítulo 3A

Nombre _____

Fecha _____

Hora _____

Guided Practice Activities 3A-4

Me gustan, me encantan (continued)

D. Complete the following sentences by writing **encanta** or **encantan**.

1. Me _____ el queso.

2. Me _____ los plátanos.

3. Me _____ los jugos.

4. Me _____ el pan.

5. Me _____ el yogur.

6. Me _____ las galletas.

E. Complete the following sentences by writing **gusta** or **gustan**.

1. ¿Te _____ las sopas?

2. No me _____ el queso.

3. No me _____ la leche.

4. No me _____ el tocino.

5. ¿Te _____ las naranjas?

6. ¿Te _____ las papas fritas?

F. Choose words from the list to complete each sentence about what you like or don't like.

el cereal	el desayuno	los huevos	las salchichas	el yogur
las hamburguesas	el jamón	el queso	el café	el té
los perritos calientes	la sopa de verduras	la pizza	las galletas	el jamón

1. Me gusta _____.

2. No me gusta _____.

3. Me gustan _____.

4. No me gustan _____.

5. ¡Me encanta _____!

6. ¡Me encantan _____!

G. Look at each drawing. Then write a sentence to say whether you like it or not. Follow the models.

Modelos _Me gustan los huevos_ . OR _No me gustan los huevos_ .

 Me gusta la pizza . OR _No me gusta la pizza_ .

1.  _____

2.  _____

3.  _____

4.  _____

Go Online WEB CODE jcd-0304
PHSchool.com

Lectura: Frutas y verduras de las Américas (pp. 168–169)

A. As you can see by its title, the reading in your textbook is about fruits and vegetables. Think about some fruits and vegetables that you eat. Write the names (in English) of three fruits and three vegetables in the spaces below.

FRUITS	VEGETABLES
_____	_____
_____	_____
_____	_____

B. Below are some Spanish words from the reading, categorized by whether they are a fruit or a vegetable. Choose the English word from the bank that you think is the best meaning for each example and write it in the blank.

potato   beans   corn   pineapple   avocado   papaya

Frutas:

1. papaya _____

2. piña _____

3. aguacate _____

Verduras:

4. papa _____

5. frijoles _____

6. maíz _____

C. On the first page of the reading you see pictures of an avocado, a mango, and a papaya. Read the information below about each fruit and answer the questions that follow.

Aguacate:
- La pulpa es fuente de energía y proteínas.
- Tiene vitaminas A y B.

Mango:
- Es originalmente de Asia.
- Tiene calcio y vitaminas A y C.

Papaya:
- Contiene mucha agua.
- Tiene más vitamina C que la naranja.

1. Which fruits have vitamin A? _____ _____

2. Which fruits have vitamin C? _____ _____

3. Which fruit is not originally from the Americas? _____

D. Look at the recipe for a **Licuado de plátano** on the second page of the reading in your textbook. If the following statements are true, circle **C** for **cierto** (*true*); if they are false, circle **F** for **falso** (*false*).

1. C F The **licuado** is a hot beverage.

2. C F A **plátano** is a banana.

3. C F Milk is used in the recipe.

4. C F The blender is called a **licuadora**.

5. C F You should blend the ingredients for 2 minutes.

Realidades Ⓐ

Capítulo 3A

Nombre _____

Fecha _____

Hora _____

Guided Practice Activities 3A-6

Presentación oral (p. 171)

Task: You and a partner will role-play a telephone conversation in Spanish between an American exchange student and a host student in Uruguay. You will each take one of the two roles and gather information about the other person.

A. You will role-play this conversation with a partner. Your role will be that of the host student. Here's how to prepare:

On a separate sheet of paper, make a list of two questions in Spanish that you might ask the exchange student. Find out:

(a) what his or her favorite activities are
(b) what he or she likes to eat and drink for breakfast (or lunch)

B. Revise your work.

1. Work with your partner to coordinate answers and to come up with a greeting and a farewell for your conversation. Here is a way to begin:

   HOST STUDENT: ¡Hola, Pablo! Soy Rosa.

   EXCHANGE STUDENT: ¡Hola, Rosa! ¿Cómo estás?

   HOST STUDENT: Bien, gracias.

2. Now, work on completing the conversation. Use filler words that you have learned and the information you have collected from **part A**. See below for a model.

   HOST STUDENT: Pues Pablo, ¿te gusta ir a la escuela?

   EXCHANGE STUDENT: Sí, me gusta mucho. Me gusta dibujar y escribir cuentos. ¿Y tú? ¿Qué te gusta hacer en la escuela?

   HOST STUDENT: A mí también me gusta ir a la escuela. Me gusta mucho correr y practicar deportes, pero no me gusta estudiar mucho. Me gusta más la hora de almuerzo. ¿Qué te gusta comer en el almuerzo?

   EXCHANGE STUDENT: Yo como un sándwich de jamón y queso o una hamburguesa. ¿Y tú?

   HOST STUDENT: A mí me encantan las ensaladas. No me gusta nada la carne. ¿Qué te gusta beber?

   EXCHANGE STUDENT: Yo bebo los refrescos todos los días. ¿Qué bebes tú?

   HOST STUDENT: A mí me gustan los jugos de frutas o bebo agua.

3. Finally, work on your ending. Look again at the **Para empezar** chapter in your textbook to get ideas for how to say good-bye. Below is a sample of how to end the conversation modeled above.

   EXCHANGE STUDENT: Bien, pues, ¡Hasta luego!

   HOST STUDENT: ¡Nos vemos!

C. You will be asked to present your conversation with your partner. The host student will go first. Listen to what your partner says and continue the conversation appropriately.

Nombre _____

Hora _____

Fecha _____

Write the Spanish vocabulary word below each picture. If there is a word or phrase, copy it in the space provided. Be sure to include the article for each noun.

la carne

los cereales

las grasas

Nombre _____

Hora _____

Fecha _____

Vocabulary Practice, Sheet 2

_____

_____

_____

_____

_____

_____

_____

_____

_____

_____

_____

_____

_____

_____

_____

_____

_____

_____

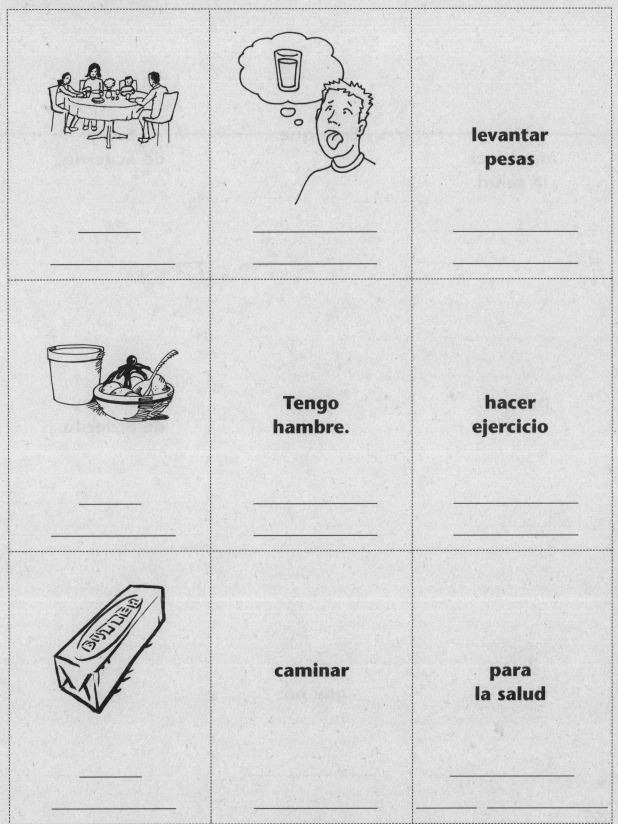

levantar pesas

Tengo hambre.

hacer ejercicio

caminar

para la salud

Realidades **A**

Capítulo 3B

Nombre _____

Hora _____

Fecha _____

Vocabulary Practice, Sheet 4

para mantener la salud _____ _____ _____ _____	**Creo que...** _____ _____	**Estoy de acuerdo.** _____ _____
prefiero _____	**Creo que sí.** _____ _____ _____	**No estoy de acuerdo.** _____ _____ _____
deber _____	**Creo que no.** _____ _____	**cada día** _____ _____

Realidades A

Capítulo 3B

Nombre _____

Hora _____

Fecha _____

Vocabulary Practice, Sheet 5

¿Por qué? _____ _____	**muchos, muchas** _____ , _____	**malo, mala** _____ , _____
porque _____	**todos, todas** _____ , _____	**sabroso, sabrosa** _____ , _____
algo _____	**horrible** _____	**prefieres** _____

Realidades A

Capítulo 3B

Nombre _____

Hora _____

Fecha _____

Vocabulary Practice, Sheet 6

hago _____	**cada día** ___ ___	**ser** _____
haces _____	___ ___	___ ___
___ ___	___ ___	___ ___

Tear out this page. Write the English words on the lines. Fold the paper along the dotted line to see the correct answers so you can check your work.

la cena _____

el bistec _____

la carne _____

el pescado _____

el pollo _____

la cebolla _____

los guisantes _____

las judías verdes _____

la lechuga _____

las papas _____

los tomates _____

las uvas _____

las zanahorias _____

el arroz _____

los cereales _____

los espaguetis _____

las grasas _____

la mantequilla _____

el helado _____

Fold In

Realidades Ⓐ

Capítulo 3B

Nombre _____

Hora _____

Fecha _____

Vocabulary Check, Sheet 2

Tear out this page. Write the Spanish words on the lines. Fold the paper along
the dotted line to see the correct answers so you can check your work.

dinner _____

beefsteak _____

meat _____

fish _____

chicken _____

onion _____

peas _____

green beans _____

lettuce _____

potatoes _____

tomatoes _____

grapes _____

carrots _____

rice _____

grains _____

spaghetti _____

fats _____

butter _____

ice cream _____

Fold In →

Realidades A

Capítulo 3B

Nombre _____

Hora _____

Fecha _____

Vocabulary Check, Sheet 3

Tear out this page. Write the English words on the lines. Fold the paper along the dotted line to see the correct answers so you can check your work.

los pasteles _____

las bebidas _____

caminar _____

hacer ejercicio _____

levantar pesas _____

para mantener _____
la salud _____

algo _____

muchos, _____
muchas

malo, mala _____

sabroso, _____
sabrosa _____

todos, _____
todas _____

Fold In

Realidades A

Capítulo 3B

Nombre _____

Hora _____

Fecha _____

Vocabulary Check, Sheet 4

Tear out this page. Write the Spanish words on the lines. Fold the paper along the dotted line to see the correct answers so you can check your work.

pastries _____

beverages _____

to walk _____

to exercise _____

to lift weights _____

to maintain
one's health _____

_____

something _____

many _____

_____

bad _____

tasty,
flavorful _____

_____

all _____

Fold In

To hear a complete list of the vocabulary for this chapter, go to Disc 1, Track 7 on the Guided Practice Audio CD, or go to www.phschool.com and type in the Web Code jcd-0399. Then click on **Repaso del capítulo.**

The plurals of adjectives (p. 190)

- Adjectives, just like definite articles, must match the noun they accompany. Singular adjectives go with singular nouns, and plural adjectives go with plural nouns.

- Adjectives that end in **-o** or **-a** must also match the noun. Masculine (**-o**) adjectives go with masculine nouns and feminine (**-a**) adjectives go with feminine nouns.

- Adjectives that end in **-e** do not change to match masculine or feminine nouns. They still change to match singular and plural nouns: **el libro interesante, las clases interesantes**.

	Definite article	Noun	Adjective
masculine singular	**el**	pan	sabros**o**
feminine singular	**la**	sopa	sabros**a**
masculine plural	**los**	jamones	sabros**os**
feminine plural	**las**	galletas	sabros**as**

A. Look at each noun. Write **M** if it is masculine or **F** if it is feminine.

1. _____ pan
2. _____ sopas
3. _____ yogur
4. _____ salchichas
5. _____ pizza

6. _____ jamón
7. _____ huevos
8. _____ quesos
9. _____ galletas
10. _____ hamburguesa

B. Now, go back to **part A**. Next to the **M** or **F** you wrote next to each noun, write **S** if the noun is singular and **P** if it is plural.

C. Here are the nouns from **part A**. Now there are adjectives with them. Circle the correct adjective form for each noun.

1. pan (**sabroso** / **sabrosos**)
2. sopas (**sabrosos** / **sabrosas**)
3. yogur (**sabrosos** / **sabroso**)
4. salchichas (**sabrosas** / **sabrosa**)
5. pizza (**sabrosos** / **sabrosa**)

6. jamón (**sabroso** / **sabrosa**)
7. huevos (**sabrosa** / **sabrosos**)
8. quesos (**sabrosos** / **sabrosas**)
9. galletas (**sabrosa** / **sabrosas**)
10. hamburguesas (**sabrosos** / **sabrosas**)

Realidades Ⓐ

Capítulo 3B

Nombre _____

Fecha _____

Hora _____

Guided Practice Activities 3B-2

The plurals of adjectives (*continued*)

D. Fill in the missing singular or plural form of each masculine adjective in the chart.

Masculine	
singular	**plural**
divertido	
simpático	
	atrevidos
	serios
artístico	

E. Now, fill in the missing singular or plural form of each feminine adjective in the chart.

Feminine	
singular	**plural**
	divertidas
simpática	
	atrevidas
seria	
	artísticas

F. Choose an adjective from the group of words. Write its correct form in the space provided.

serio	seria	serios	serias
atrevido	atrevida	atrevidos	atrevidas
artístico	artística	artísticos	artísticas

1. Laura y Elena estudian mucho. Son _____.

2. Sandra monta en monopatín. Es _____.

3. Mario dibuja. Es _____.

4. Tomás y Beatriz trabajan mucho. Son _____.

5. Lorenzo y Fernando esquían. Son _____.

Go Online WEB CODE jcd-0313
PHSchool.com

The verb *ser* (p. 192)

- You have already learned and used some forms of the verb **ser**, which means *to be*:

  Yo soy serio. Tú eres simpática. Ella es artística.

- **Ser** is an irregular verb. You will need to memorize its forms.

yo	**soy**	nosotros/nosotras	**somos**
tú	**eres**	vosotros/vosotras	**sois**
usted/él/ella	**es**	ustedes/ellos/ellas	**son**

A. Choose the correct subject pronoun for each form of **ser** and circle it.

1. (yo / él) es
2. (ustedes / ella) son
3. (tú / ella) eres
4. (ella / yo) es

5. (usted / tú) es
6. (nosotros / ellas) son
7. (ellos / nosotros) somos
8. (yo / él) soy

B. Now, write the correct form of **ser** next to each subject pronoun.

1. tú _____
2. usted _____
3. ellos _____
4. él _____

5. ellas _____
6. nosotras _____
7. yo _____
8. ustedes _____

C. Complete the exchanges by writing in the correct form of **ser**.

1. VERA: Yo _____ estudiante. ¿Y tú?

   GONZALO: Yo _____ estudiante también.

2. PABLO: Tú _____ muy deportista, ¿no?

   ENRIQUE: Sí, pero yo también _____ muy estudioso.

3. INÉS: Susana y Olivia _____ muy divertidas.

   MARCOS: Sí. Olivia _____ muy simpática también.

4. PACO Y LUIS: Nosotros _____ perezosos. No estudiamos mucho.

   ANA: Bueno, yo _____ muy trabajadora. Me gusta estudiar.

The verb *ser* (*continued*)

D. Look at each drawing. Complete the question with a form of **ser**. Follow the model.

| Modelo |

¿Cómo _____*es*_____ él?

1. ¿Cómo _____ él?

2. ¿Cómo _____ tú?

3. ¿Cómo _____ ellas?

4. ¿Cómo _____ nosotras?

5. ¿Cómo _____ yo?

E. Now, complete each sentence with the correct form of **ser** and the correct adjective ending. Refer back to the art in **part D**. Follow the model.

| Modelo | Él _____*es*_____ simpático_____.

1. Él _____ artístic_____.

2. Tú _____ perezos_____.

3. Ellas _____ estudios_____.

4. Nosotras _____ inteligente_____.

5. Yo _____ atrevid_____.

Lectura: La comida de los atletas (pp. 198–199)

> Skimming is a useful technique to help you get through a reading. You think of general information that you are looking for. Then you quickly read the words to find it.

A. List three things you would expect to find in an article about an athlete's eating habits.

1. _____
2. _____
3. _____

B. Skim the article and check off the things in your list from **part A** that you find.

C. Note that the pie chart in your textbook shows how much of an athlete's diet can be divided into three categories. Next to each category below, write the English translation of the word. Then fill in the percentage number according to the pie chart.

	English	**Number**
1. carbohidratos	_____	_____ %
2. proteínas	_____	_____ %
3. grasas	_____	_____ %

D. The reading in your textbook gives a picture and a short description of what foods are good for each big meal of the day. Next to each food given below circle whether the reading says it is best for **D (desayuno)**, **A (almuerzo)**, or **C (cena)**.

1. **D A C**   pan con mantequilla   4. **D A C**   papas

2. **D A C**   pasta   5. **D A C**   jalea

3. **D A C**   yogur

E. Read the selection below and answer the questions that follow.

> *La noche antes del partido, el jugador bebe un litro de jugo de naranja, y durante el partido bebe hasta dos litros de agua y bebidas deportivas.*

1. Circle the three kinds of drinks mentioned in the reading.

2. What is a *litro* in English? _____

3. When does the player drink a *litro* of orange juice? _____

Realidades A

Capítulo 3B

Nombre _____

Hora _____

Fecha _____

Guided Practice Activities 3B-6

Presentación escrita (p. 201)

Task: You will make a poster in Spanish with three suggestions for better health. You will need to research what are proven good eating and exercise habits.

1 Prewrite. Talk to classmates, teachers, the school nurse, or your parents about good eating and exercise habits, especially for teens. Then list their ideas under the following headings to help you organize your information:

- Debes comer _____.
- No debes comer mucho(a) _____.
- Debes beber _____.
- No debes beber mucho(a) _____.
- Debes _____ para mantener la salud.

2 Draft. Create your first draft on a separate sheet of paper. (You do not need to use posterboard for this draft.) List your ideas from the prewrite stage. Organize them in a neat or artistic way. Sketch out the visuals you want to include on the poster.

3 Revise.

A. Someone else will check your work for the following:

_____ Have you communicated the three suggestions well?

_____ Do the visuals help with the meaning?

_____ Will the visuals make the poster attractive?

_____ Are all words spelled correctly?

_____ Are grammar and vocabulary used correctly?

B. Rewrite your poster using the person's suggestions.

4 Publish. Your final draft will be on some sort of posterboard. You will want to carefully add any illustrations and designs you had sketched out in an earlier stage.

5 Evaluate. Your teacher will tell you how your poster will be graded. Your teacher will check:

- your completion of the task
- the accuracy of your vocabulary and grammar
- your effective use of visuals

Realidades (A)

Capítulo 4A

Nombre _____

Hora _____

Fecha _____

Vocabulary Flash Cards, Sheet 1

Write the Spanish vocabulary word below each picture. If there is a word or phrase, copy it in the space provided. Be sure to include the article for each noun.

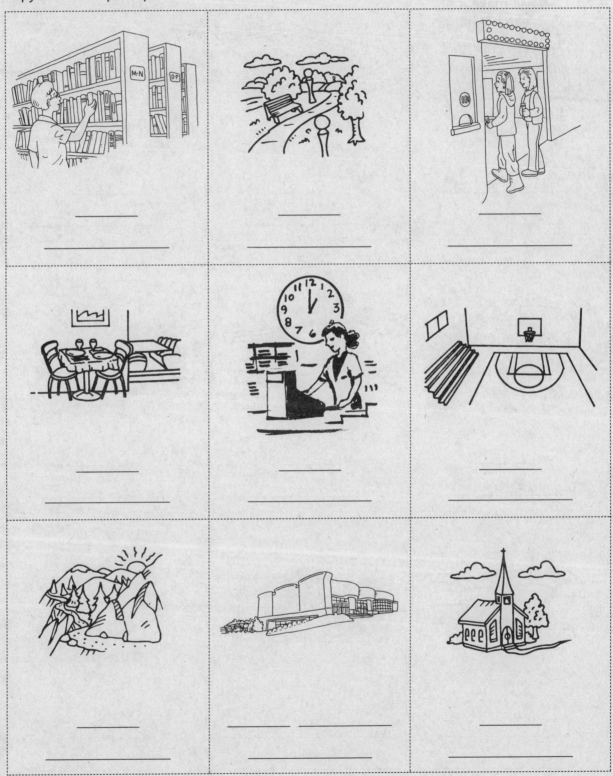

Realidades **A**

Capítulo 4A

Nombre _____

Fecha _____

Hora _____

Vocabulary Flash Cards, Sheet 2

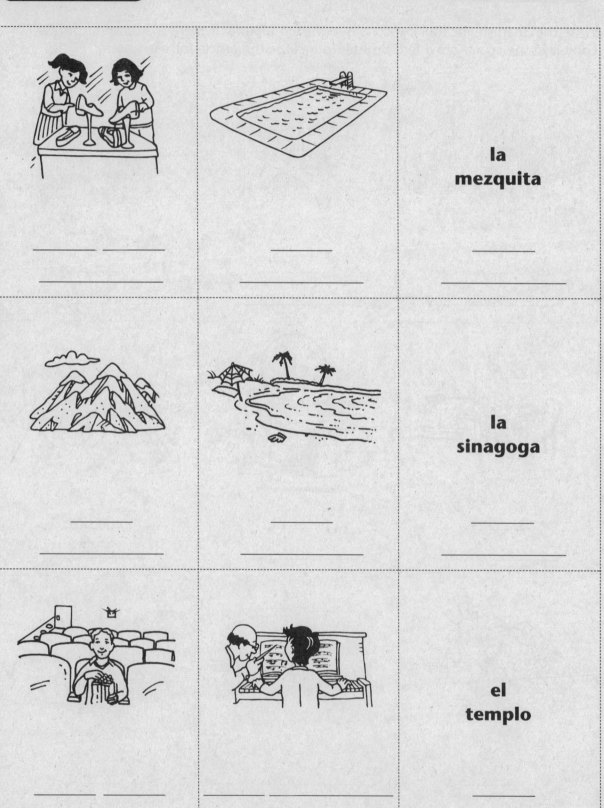

la
mezquita

_____

la
sinagoga

_____

el
templo

_____

Realidades A

Capítulo 4A

Nombre _____

Hora _____

Fecha _____

Vocabulary Flash Cards, Sheet 3

la
casa

_____

_____

Me quedo
en casa.

_____ _____

_____

¿Adónde?

_____

en
casa

_____

_____

a

_____

¿Con
quién?

a
casa

_____

_____

el
restaurante

_____

_____

a la,
al

_____,

_____

¿Con
quién?

_____

_____

Realidades **A**

Capítulo 4A

Nombre _____

Hora _____

Fecha _____

Vocabulary Flash Cards, Sheet 4

con mis amigos

_____ _____

_____

¿Cuándo?

_____

los fines de semana

_____ _____

_____ _____

con mis / tus amigos

_____ _____

_____

después

_____

los lunes, los martes ...

_____

_____

solo, sola

_____,

_____

después de

_____

_____

tiempo libre

_____

_____

Realidades Ⓐ

Capítulo 4A

Nombre

Hora

Fecha

Vocabulary Flash Cards, Sheet 5

de

¡No me digas!

¿De dónde eres?

para

generalmente

Realidades (A)

Capítulo 4A

Nombre

Hora

Fecha

Vocabulary Flash Cards, Sheet 6

Realidades Ⓐ

Capítulo 4A

Nombre _____

Hora _____

Fecha _____

Vocabulary Check, Sheet 1

Tear out this page. Write the English words on the lines. Fold the paper along the dotted line to see the correct answers so you can check your work.

ir de compras   _____

ver una
película   _____

la lección de
piano   _____

     _____

la biblioteca   _____

el café   _____

el campo   _____

en casa   _____

el centro
comercial   _____

el cine   _____

el gimnasio   _____

la iglesia   _____

la mezquita   _____

las montañas   _____

el parque   _____

la piscina   _____

la playa   _____

el restaurante   _____

Fold In

Tear out this page. Write the Spanish words on the lines. Fold the paper along the dotted line to see the correct answers so you can check your work.

to go shopping _____

to see a movie _____

_____

piano lesson
(class) _____

_____

library _____

café _____

countryside _____

at home _____

mall _____

_____

movie theater _____

gym _____

church _____

mosque _____

mountains _____

park _____

swimming pool _____

beach _____

restaurant _____

Fold In ←

Realidades Ⓐ

Capítulo 4A

Nombre _____

Fecha _____

Hora _____

Vocabulary Check, Sheet 3

Tear out this page. Write the English words on the lines. Fold the paper along the dotted line to see the correct answers so you can check your work.

la sinagoga _____

el templo _____

_____

el trabajo _____

solo, sola _____

¿Cuándo? _____

después _____

después (de) _____

los fines de _____
semana

los lunes, los _____
martes... _____

tiempo libre _____

Fold In →

Tear out this page. Write the Spanish words on the lines. Fold the paper along the dotted line to see the correct answers so you can check your work.

synagogue   _____

temple,   _____
Protestant church

work, job   _____

alone   _____

When?   _____

afterwards   _____

after   _____

on weekends   _____

                           _____

on Mondays,   _____
on Tuesdays . . .
                           _____

free time   _____

Fold In

To hear a complete list of the vocabulary for this chapter, go to Disc 1, Track 8 on the Guided Practice Audio CD, or go to www.phschool.com and type in the Web Code jcd-0489. Then click on **Repaso del capítulo.**

Realidades Ⓐ

Capítulo 4A

Nombre _____

Fecha _____

Hora _____

Guided Practice Activities 4A-1

The verb *ir* (p. 218)

- The verb **ir** means "to go." It is irregular. Here are its forms.

yo	**voy**	nosotros/nosotras	**vamos**
tú	**vas**	vosotros/vosotras	**vais**
usted/él/ella	**va**	ustedes/ellos/ellas	**van**

- **¡Vamos!** means "Let's go!"

A. Choose the correct subject pronoun for each form of **ir** and circle it.

1. (**tú** / **él**) va

2. (**yo** / **usted**) voy

3. (**ellas** / **nosotras**) vamos

4. (**usted** / **ustedes**) va

5. (**ustedes** / **él**) van

6. (**tú** / **yo**) vas

7. (**ellos** / **ella**) van

8. (**yo** / **ella**) va

B. Now, write the correct form of **ir** next to each subject pronoun.

1. ella _____

2. ustedes _____

3. yo _____

4. nosotros _____

5. tú _____

6. él _____

7. ellos _____

8. usted _____

C. Complete each sentence by writing in the correct form of **ir**.

1. Yo _____ al cine para ver una película.

2. Ellas _____ al parque para correr.

3. Nosotros _____ al gimnasio para levantar pesas.

4. Tú _____ al restaurante para comer.

5. Ella _____ a la piscina para nadar.

The verb *ir* (*continued*)

▌ • When **ir** + **a** is followed by the definite article **el**, **a** + **el** combines to form **al**:

(**vamos** *a*) + (*el* **parque**) = **Vamos** *al* **parque.**

D. Complete each sentence by writing a form of **ir** + **al** or **a la**. Remember to use **al** when the noun after the write-on line is masculine. Use **a la** when the noun is feminine. Follow the models.

Modelos Ellos _____*van al*_____ parque.

Ellos _____*van a la*_____ oficina.

1. Silvia _____ casa.

2. Cristina y María _____ café.

3. Tú _____ playa.

4. Nosotros _____ parque.

5. Usted _____ campo.

6. Yo _____ piscina.

▌ • To ask where someone is going, use **¿Adónde?** as in: **¿Adónde vas?**
▌ • To answer, use forms of **ir** + **a** as in: **Voy a la oficina.**

E. Complete the following exchanges by finishing the second sentence with a form of **ir** and the place indicated. Follow the model.

Modelo

el cine

—¿Adónde vas?

—Yo ____*voy al cine*____.

1.

el parque

—¿Adónde vamos?

—Nosotros _____.

2.

el gimnasio

—¿Adónde van?

—Ellas _____.

3.

la piscina

—¿Adónde va?

—Él _____.

4.

la iglesia

—¿Adónde voy?

—Tú _____.

Go Online WEB CODE jcd-0403
PHSchool.com

Realidades Ⓐ

Capítulo 4A

Nombre _____

Hora _____

Fecha _____

Guided Practice Activities 4A-3

Asking questions (p. 224)

- Interrogatives are words that you use to ask questions. Here are some Spanish interrogatives.

Categories	Interrogatives		
People	¿Quién?	¿Con quién?	
Location	¿Dónde?	¿Adónde?	¿De dónde?
Things or actions	¿Qué?	¿Cuál?	¿Cuántos? / ¿Cuántas?
Reason	¿Por qué?		
Time	¿Cuándo?		
Description (how)	¿Cómo?		

- You can change a statement into a question by raising your voice at the end:

  ¿**Margarita va a la biblioteca?** In this case, you do not use an interrogative.

- These kinds of questions expect the answer will be *yes* or *no*. You can add ¿**verdad?** (*right?*) to the end to emphasize this: **Margarita va a la biblioteca, ¿verdad?**

A. Each drawing or group of drawings represents a question category in the chart above. Write the interrogatives that go with each group. Follow the model.

Modelo

`8:52` ─ ¿ _____Cuándo_____ ?

1.

2.
   Yo

3.

_____

_____

_____

_____

Realidades Ⓐ

Capítulo 4A

Nombre _____

Fecha _____

Hora _____

Guided Practice Activities 4A-4

Asking questions (*continued*)

• In Spanish questions with interrogatives, the verb comes before the subject:
¿Adónde va Margarita?

B. Look at the following groups of exchanges. Write in the correct interrogative to complete each exchange. Use the interrogatives listed for each group.

Location: *¿Dónde? ¿Adónde?*

1. —¿_____ van Natalia y Roberto?
   —Van a la biblioteca para estudiar.

2. —¿_____ levantas pesas?
   — Levanto pesas en el gimnasio.

People: *¿Quién? ¿Con quién?*

3. —¿_____ hablas mucho por teléfono?
   —Hablo mucho con mi amiga Tina. Ella es muy divertida.

4. —¿_____ es su profesor de español?
   — Es la señora Oliveros. Es muy inteligente.

Things: *¿Qué? ¿Cuántos?*

5. —¿_____ libros hay en la biblioteca?
   —¡Hay muchos!

6. —¿_____ comes para el desayuno?
   —Como pan tostado y tocino.

Reason and Description: *¿Por qué? ¿Cómo?*

7. —¿_____ estudias tanto?
   — Soy muy trabajadora y me gusta leer.

8. —¿_____ es la clase de matemáticas?
   — Es interesante, pero difícil.

Go Online WEB CODE jcd-0404
PHSchool.com

Realidades A

Capítulo 4A

Nombre _____

Hora _____

Fecha _____

Guided Practice Activities 4A-5

Asking questions (*continued*)

C. Look at each group of phrases. Put them in order to form a question by numbering each group 1, 2, or 3. Then write them in order on the write-on line below. Follow the model. You can also look at the questions in **part B** for examples.

Modelo	Paulina / adónde / va
	3 1 2

¿ _____*Adónde va Paulina*_____ ?

1. es / el profesor de español / quién

_____

2. sillas / hay / cuántas

_____

3. Luisa / adónde / va

_____

4. cómo / ella / es

_____

5. corren / dónde / ellos

_____

6. con quién / habla / Margarita

_____

Realidades **A**

Capítulo 4A

Nombre _____

Hora _____

Fecha _____

Guided Practice Activities 4A-6

Lectura: Al centro comercial (pp. 230–231)

A. List four events that you think would take place at a special-event week in a shopping center near you.

1. _____   3. _____

2. _____   4. _____

B. According to the reading in your book, what are the dates for the event week at the Plaza del Sol? Write the answers in English below, next to the days of the week you are given.

Monday, _____   Friday, _____

Tuesday, _____   Saturday, _____

Wednesday, _____   Sunday, _____

Thursday, _____

C. Look at the word bank below. Choose which expression in English best matches with the words you are given and write it in the spaces provided.

Andean music	**Yoga class**	**Evening of jazz**
Evening of tango	**Photography show**	**Yoga performance**

1. Música andina   _____

2. Clase de yoga   _____

3. Noche de jazz   _____

4. Exposición de fotografía _____

5. Exhibición de yoga   _____

6. Noche de tango   _____

D. Read the description of Andean music and answer the questions that follow.

‖ *El grupo Sol Andino toca música andina fusionada con bossa nova y jazz el lunes a las 8.00 P.M. Abierto al público.* ‖

1. Circle the name of the group in the paragraph above.

2. What does this group fuse with its brand of Andean music?

_____ and _____

3. Can the public attend this show? _____

Go Online WEB CODE jcd-0405
PHSchool.com

Realidades A

Capítulo 4A

Nombre _____

Hora _____

Fecha _____

Guided Practice Activities 4A-7

Lectura: Al centro comercial (*continued*)

E. Read the description of the yoga class and answer the questions that follow.

> *La práctica de yoga es todos los martes desde las 7.00 hasta las 9.00 P.M. La instructora Lucía Gómez Paloma enseña los secretos de esta disciplina. Inscríbase al teléfono 224-24-16. Vacantes limitadas.*

1. How long does the yoga class last? _____

2. What does the sequence of numbers 224-24-16 stand for? _____

3. Can anyone attend this class? _____

   Why or why not? _____

F. After looking through the readings in your textbook, you know that four events are explained in detail. These events are listed below. You must choose which event goes with the descriptions you are given. Write the name of the event in the space provided.

Música andina	Clase de yoga	Sábado flamenco	Clase de repostería

1. _____ instructora Lucía Gómez Paloma

2. _____ guitarrista Ernesto Hermoza

3. _____ grupo Sol Andino

4. _____ la Repostería Ideal

5. _____ maestro Rudolfo Torres

6. _____ es el sábado a las 8.00 P.M.

Realidades Ⓐ

Capítulo 4A

Nombre _____

Fecha _____

Hora _____

Guided Practice Activities 4A-8

Presentación oral (p. 233)

Task: You and a partner will play the roles of a new student and a student who has been at school for awhile. This student must find out about the new student.

A. You will need to prepare the role of the student who has been at the school for awhile. On a separate sheet of paper, make a list of four questions you have for the new student. Then, think of a greeting to introduce yourself.

First question: Find out where the new student is from.

Second question: Find out what activities the new student likes to do.

Third question: Find out on what days of the week the student likes to do things.

Fourth question: Find out with whom the new student does these activities.

B. You will need to practice your conversation.

1. First, work on the greeting. See below for a model.

EXPERIENCED STUDENT:	¡Hola, amigo! Soy Ana María. ¿Cómo te llamas?
NEW STUDENT:	Me llamo Miguel Ángel.

2. Now, you will need to put together your questions and answers in a conversation. Use the following as a model:

EXPERIENCED STUDENT:	¿De dónde eres, Miguel Ángel?
NEW STUDENT:	Soy de Barranquilla, Colombia.
EXPERIENCED STUDENT:	Bien. ¿Qué te gusta hacer en tu tiempo libre?
NEW STUDENT:	Me gusta ir al campo, nadar en el mar y caminar en las montañas.
EXPERIENCED STUDENT:	A mí también me gusta ir al campo. ¿Cuándo vas tú al campo?
NEW STUDENT:	Voy al campo los fines de semana. Me gusta caminar cuando estoy de vacaciones.
EXPERIENCED STUDENT:	¿Y con quién vas al campo o a las montañas?
NEW STUDENT:	Voy con mi familia.

3. Now work on a closing. Use the following as a model:

EXPERIENCED STUDENT:	¡Bueno, hasta luego Miguel Ángel!
NEW STUDENT:	¡Nos vemos, Ana María!

C. You will need to present your conversation. Make sure you do the following in your presentation:

_____ provide and obtain all the necessary information

_____ have no breaks in the conversation

_____ speak clearly

Realidades Ⓐ

Capítulo 4B

Nombre _____

Fecha _____

Hora _____

Vocabulary Practice, Sheet 1

Write the Spanish vocabulary word below each picture. If there is a word or phrase, copy it in the space provided. Be sure to include the article for each noun.

Realidades **A**

Capítulo 4B

Nombre _____

Hora _____

Fecha _____

Vocabulary Practice, Sheet 2

_____

_____

_____ ,

_____

_____ ,

_____

_____ ,

_____

(yo) sé

_____ _____

_____

_____

(tú) sabes

_____

contento, contenta _____ , _____	¿A qué hora? _____ _____ _____	de la mañana _____ _____ _____
enfermo, enferma _____ , _____	a la una _____ _____ _____	de la noche _____ _____ _____
mal _____ _____ _____	a las ocho _____ _____ _____	de la tarde _____ _____ _____

Realidades A

Capítulo 4B

Nombre _____

Hora _____

Fecha _____

Vocabulary Practice, Sheet 4

este fin de semana	**conmigo**	**¡Ay! ¡Qué pena!**
_____ _____ _____ _____	 _____	_____ _____ _____
esta noche	**contigo**	**¡Genial!**
   _____ _____	 _____	 _____
esta tarde	**(yo) puedo**	**¡Qué buena idea!**
   _____ _____	 _____	_____ _____

Realidades Ⓐ

Capítulo 4B

Nombre _____

Fecha _____

Hora _____

Vocabulary Practice, Sheet 5

¡Oye!

_____

¿Te gustaría?

_____

_____

demasiado

_____

lo siento

_____

_____

me gustaría

_____

_____

entonces

_____

(yo) quiero

_____

_____

Tengo que...

_____

un poco (de)

_____ _____

Realidades Ⓐ

Capítulo 4B

Nombre

Fecha

Hora

Vocabulary Practice, Sheet 6

**(tú)
puedes**

_____

_____

**(tú)
quieres**

_____

_____

**ir a +
infinitive**

_____ _____

_____

_____

_____

_____

_____

_____

_____

_____

_____

_____

_____

_____

_____

_____

Tear out this page. Write the English words on the lines. Fold the paper along the dotted line to see the correct answers so you can check your work.

el baile _____

el concierto _____

la fiesta _____

el partido _____

ir de cámping _____

ir de pesca _____

jugar al
básquetbol _____
_____

jugar al béisbol _____

jugar al fútbol _____

jugar al fútbol
americano _____

jugar al golf _____

jugar al tenis _____

jugar al
vóleibol _____
_____

cansado,
cansada _____

contento,
contenta _____

Fold In

Realidades Ⓐ

Capítulo 4B

Nombre _____

Hora _____

Fecha _____

Vocabulary Check, Sheet 2

Tear out this page. Write the Spanish words on the lines. Fold the paper along the dotted line to see the correct answers so you can check your work.

dance _____

concert _____

party _____

game, match _____

to go camping _____

to go fishing _____

to play
basketball _____
_____

to play baseball _____

to play soccer _____

to play football _____
_____

to play golf _____

to play tennis _____

to play
volleyball _____
_____

tired _____
_____

happy _____
_____

Fold In ←

Tear out this page. Write the English words on the lines. Fold the paper along the dotted line to see the correct answers so you can check your work.

enfermo, _____
enferma

ocupado, _____
ocupada

triste _____

a la una _____

de la mañana _____

de la noche _____

_____

de la tarde _____

este fin de _____
semana

esta noche _____

esta tarde _____

¡Ay! ¡Qué pena! _____

¡Genial! _____

lo siento _____

¡Qué buena idea! _____

Fold In

Nombre _____

Hora _____

Fecha _____

Vocabulary Check, Sheet 4

Tear out this page. Write the Spanish words on the lines. Fold the paper along the dotted line to see the correct answers so you can check your work.

sick _____

_____

busy _____

_____

sad _____

at one (o'clock) _____

in the morning _____

in the evening, _____
at night

in the afternoon _____

this weekend _____

_____

this evening _____

this afternoon _____

Oh! What a shame! _____

Great! _____

I'm sorry _____

What a good idea! _____

Fold In

To hear a complete list of the vocabulary for this chapter, go to Disc 1, Track 9 on the Guided Practice Audio CD, or go to www.phschool.com and type in the Web Code jcd-0499. Then click on **Repaso del capítulo.**

Realidades Ⓐ

Capítulo 4B

Nombre _____

Hora _____

Fecha _____

Guided Practice Activities 4B-1

Ir + a + infinitive (p. 252)

- You have already learned to use the verb **ir** (*to go*). To review, here are its forms, which are irregular.

yo	**voy**	nosotros/nosotras	**vamos**
tú	**vas**	vosotros/vosotras	**vais**
usted/él/ella	**va**	ustedes/ellos/ellas	**van**

- As you have learned, the infinitive is the basic form of the verb (**hablar, comer, leer,** etc.). It is equivalent to "to . . ." in English: *to talk, to eat, to read.*

- When you use **ir + a** with an infinitive, it means you or others are *going to do something* in the future. It is the same as "I am going to . . ." in English: **Voy a leer el libro. Vamos a ver la película.**

A. Review by writing the correct form of **ir** next to each subject pronoun.

1. tú _____

2. ellos _____

3. él _____

4. usted _____

5. ella _____

6. yo _____

7. ustedes _____

8. nosotras _____

B. Now complete each sentence with the correct form of **ir.**

1. Marta y Rosa _____ a estudiar esta tarde.

2. Yo _____ a jugar al tenis esta tarde.

3. Tú _____ a montar en monopatín mañana.

4. Nosotras _____ a bailar mañana.

5. Ustedes _____ a correr esta tarde.

6. Serena _____ a ir de cámping mañana.

C. Complete the exchanges with the correct form of **ir.**

1. LAURA: ¿Qué _____ a hacer este fin de semana?

   CARLOS: Yo _____ a jugar al golf.

2. ANA: ¿Qué _____ a hacer ustedes mañana?

   TOMÁS: Nosotros _____ a trabajar.

3. ERNESTO: ¿Qué _____ a hacer Susana hoy?

   RICARDO: Ella y yo _____ a ir al cine.

Ir + a + infinitive (continued)

D. Write questions with **ir** + **a** + **hacer**. Follow the models.

Modelos   (tú) / hacer hoy

¿Qué _____*vas a hacer hoy*_____?

(ellos) / hacer este fin de semana

¿Qué _____*van a hacer este fin de semana*_____?

1. yo / hacer esta tarde

¿Qué _____?

2. nosotros / hacer mañana

¿Qué _____?

3. ustedes / hacer hoy

¿Qué _____?

4. tú / hacer este fin de semana

¿Qué _____?

5. ella / hacer esta mañana

¿Qué _____?

E. Write sentences to say what the people shown are going to do tomorrow. Follow the model.

Modelo   Roberto

  Roberto va a jugar al béisbol.

1.   Ana

  _____

2.   Juan y José

  _____

3.   tú

  _____

4.   yo

  _____

Go ⬤**nline** WEB CODE jcd-0413
PHSchool.com

The verb *jugar* (p. 256)

- **Jugar** (*to play a sport or game*) uses the regular **-ar** present tense endings.
- However, **jugar** does not use the same stem in all its forms. **Jugar** is a *stem-changing verb*. In most forms, it uses **jueg-** + the **-ar** endings. But in the **nosotros/nosotras, vosotros/vosotras** forms, it uses **jug-** + the **-ar** endings.
- Here are the forms of **jugar**:

yo	**juego**	nosotros/nosotras	**jugamos**
tú	**juegas**	vosotros/vosotras	**jugáis**
usted/él/ella	**juega**	ustedes/ellos/ellas	**juegan**

A. Circle the forms of **jugar** in each sentence. Underline the stem in each form of **jugar**.

1. Yo juego al tenis este fin de semana.

2. Ellos juegan al básquetbol esta noche.

3. Nosotros jugamos videojuegos mañana.

4. Ustedes juegan al golf este fin de semana.

5. Tú y yo jugamos al béisbol esta tarde.

6. Tú juegas al fútbol americano este fin de semana.

7. Ella juega al fútbol esta tarde.

8. Nosotras jugamos al vóleibol hoy.

B. Now, write the forms of **jugar** you circled in **part A**. Put them in the corresponding rows of the table. The first one has been done for you.

Subject pronoun	Form of *jugar*
1. yo	*juego*
2. ellos	
3. nosotros	
4. ustedes	
5. tú y yo	
6. tú	
7. ella	
8. nosotras	

Realidades Ⓐ

Capítulo 4B

Nombre _____

Hora _____

Fecha _____

Guided Practice Activities 4B-4

The verb *jugar* (*continued*)

C. Write questions with **jugar**. Follow the model.

Modelo	usted

_____*¿A qué juega?*_____

1. tú

   _____

2. nosotros

   _____

3. yo

   _____

4. ella

   _____

5. tú y yo

   _____

6. ustedes

   _____

D. Now write sentences to say what people are playing. Follow the model.

Modelo

 Eduardo

_____*Eduardo juega al fútbol.*_____

1. Rosa y Ana

   _____

2. nosotros

   _____

3. yo

   _____

4. tú

   _____

5. ustedes

   _____

Go Online WEB CODE jcd-0414
PHSchool.com

Lectura: Sergio y Lorena: El futuro de golf (pp. 260–261)

A. A list of personal information is given about each golfer in your textbook reading. Below are several of the categories for each piece of information. Write what you think is the English word for each category below.

1. Nombre _____

2. Fecha de nacimiento _____

3. Lugar de nacimiento _____

4. Su objetivo _____

5. Profesional _____

6. Universidad _____

B. Look at the list of **aficiones** (*interests*) for each golfer below. Then, answer the questions that follow.

SERGIO: Real Madrid, tenis, fútbol, videojuegos

LORENA: básquetbol, tenis, bicicleta de montaña, correr, nadar, comida italiana

1. What one interest do both golfers share? _____

2. What interest does Sergio have that is not a sport? _____

3. What interest does Lorena have that is not a sport? _____

C. Look at the following sentences from the reading. Circle **S** if they are about Sergio and **L** if they are about Lorena.

1. S L Juega para el Club de Campo del Mediterráneo en Borriol.

2. S L Es la mejor golfista de México.

3. S L Su padre Víctor es golfista profesional.

4. S L Tiene el nombre "El niño."

5. S L Quiere ser la golfista número uno.

6. S L A la edad de 17 años gana su primer torneo de profesionales.

D. Now, answer the questions about the two golfers from the reading. Write in either **Lorena, Sergio,** or **both** depending on the best answer.

1. Who was born in 1980? _____

2. Who is from Spain? _____

3. Who likes soccer? _____

4. Who likes tennis? _____

5. Who went to the University of Arizona? _____

6. Who wants to be the best golfer in the world? _____

Realidades Ⓐ

Capítulo 4B

Nombre _____

Hora _____

Fecha _____

Guided Practice Activities 4B-6

Presentación escrita (p. 263)

Task: Pretend you want to invite a friend to an upcoming special event on your calendar. You will need to write one invitation to that friend and anyone else you want to invite.

❶ Prewrite. Think about what event you want to attend. Fill in the information below about the event.

Name of event: _____

When (day and time): _____

Where: _____

Who is going: _____

❷ Draft. Use the information from step 1 to write a first draft of your invitation on a separate sheet of paper. See below for a model.

> ¡Hola amigos!
>   Quiero invitarlos a una noche de baile caribeño en la sala de reuniones de la iglesia. La fiesta va a ser de las siete de la tarde hasta las once de la noche, el viernes, el cinco de mayo.
>   Quiero verlos a todos ustedes allí.
> Su amiga,
> Melisa

❸ Revise.

A. Read your note and check for the following:

_____ Is the spelling correct? (Consult a dictionary if you are not sure.)

_____ Did you use verbs correctly?

_____ Is all the necessary information included?

_____ Is there anything you should add or change?

B. Rewrite your invitation if there were any problems.

❹ Publish. Write a final copy of your invitation, making any necessary changes. Be sure to write or type neatly, as others will need to read your writing. You may also add a border decoration.

Notes

Notes